*R*evelations *O*n *L*onging *S*treet

Louisa Loveridge-Gallas

Revelations On Longing Street

Louisa Loveridge-Gallas

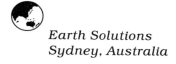

Earth Solutions
Sydney, Australia

Publisher
Earth Solutions
Sydney, Australia
earthsolutions@yahoo.com

First published 1998

Designed by Mary Lou Lamonda
Drawings and Cover by Louisa Loveridge-Gallas with
exception of Wood Stove drawing by Richard Gallas
Back cover photo by Robin Replogle
Printed by Image Systems

National Library of Australia
Cataloguing-in-Publication data:

Loveridge-Gallas, Louisa
Revelations On Longing Street
ISBN 0 9585493 0 3

These poems originally appeared in the following publications:
Cream City Review - "Late In The Season"; *Wisconsin
Magazine, Milwaukee Journal* - "The Starwheel"; *Wisconsin
Poets Calendar* - "Clark Street Moon"; Shepherd Express - "Old
Louie Schultz," The Near Miss"; *The Five Petalled Blossom:
Feminist Writers' Guild Anthology*- "Divining"; *Poetry Review*-
"Old Woman Earth"; *Hodge Podge Poetry* - "For Angela Who
Is Beyond"; *Illinois State University's Humanities Curriculum*-
"The Body Radiant"

Dedication

To the muse,
and
to life:
this hard yet
singing road.

To Ester,
I hope you will
love these poems as
do. Susan

To Esty,
Love to you Esty.
please come see me.
love,
Lorin

Gratitude

This book owes its life and form to Mary Lou Lamonda of Earth Solutions who grasped these poems and stories by the hand and put firm earth beneath them. Without her this work would still be white caps on the tossing sea of my creative chaos. I can't express enough my admiration for her publishing expertise in this age of high tech lay-out and printing; her aesthetic judgment, poetic ear and the endurance of a steadfast angel.

I want to express my endless love and respect for my mentor, husband and "most reliable wildlife," Richard, who has so many gifts. He's been an anchor, yet full of adventure, and always encouraged my work, critiquing it with a great talent for spotting a false note and under-developed lines and characters.

My deep gratitude to Chris Uihlein for his generous support; also to Sara and Lou Gallas for their love and contribution.

I am grateful for my participation in the Wisconsin Arts Board's Artist in Residency and Education Program for teaching and writing opportunities, 1985-1989; as well as Art Reach, Milwaukee, and ArtsWorld.

Thank you, forever, to Claudia Schmidt, for her support, the creative opportunities and grace she offered to me as a performer, including bringing my piano out of the mothballs; and over the years her inclusion in concerts of "The Body Radiant" and "Ode to Mud."

Love always to my Aunt Jetti and Uncle Lou for their abiding love and loyalty even in my hardest years that defied understanding.

Thanks to Ro Hanus for her technical and artistic support and Dan Sargeant for his scrupulous copy editing. To Heidi Cornehls for her loving inspiration—her big hearted ability to reach for "the big picture" and the best in everyone. Thank you, Tahnahga, and those who passed on to you, the deep experience that everything is alive and related on this Earth.

My deep love and appreciation to all of my friends for your support through all these years!

Street Directory

In The Neighborhood

Belonging To The Body

A SOFT PLACE TO FALL

FAMILY

THE KINDLY APOCALYPSE

The Long Slide Home

Come To Me

First off,
you will not always
find me beautiful!

Sometimes I happen
fast,
and fierce,
with hot breath
and urgent hands
making you live each day
as if your hair were on fire.

I ride the backs of refugees,
sink into the reveries
of bees
smeared with pollen,
then embrace the celibate
ecstasy of saints.

Do you know who I am?

I'm not always clear
or uplifting,
I may tear you up
like war stinking in
young boy's wounds.
I am free
and speak in tongues,
I walk everywhere
and come back from the unspoken
with all the details.

No one owns me.

Do you notice how I
have a woman's body,
yet reveal a man's also,
come, find me
beyond anatomy!

Sometimes I have the body
of the moon,
who has high hopes,
again and again retrieving
losses
from the jaws
of dragon night,
over and over,
the moon trusts,
fills and fills
until she says, *"YES!"*

Now, do you know me?

Come close,
and call to me,
some call me poetry,
the muse,
Oh, I have moods,
I meditate in forests
celebrating anything,
the rivermoonbird dawn aha!
Then spin around
to regret
everything—
the one that got away,
the life unblossomed,
the knot in the heart
never pierced.

I can be tasteful,
make love
with scented touch
and delicate sounds,
with room service far below
waiting to bring up
tiny cucumber sandwiches
without crusts,
and little finger bowls after.

But *only for so long*
when I must break out,
tug at your soul,
press against your cool heart!

Call me common,
call me divine,
just let me grasp you close,
whispering,
"Come to me,
I am the vowels of your
deepest nakedness,
full of heat,
I'll go the distance for you
like revelations
on Longing Street!"

Into The Belly Of Time

How do we slip
  out of eternity
   into the belly
    of a woman?

All of our atoms
have lived before, before now,
even before BEFORE,
as stars, or mud,
as stone, or the unnameable,

again, again, changed, transformed,
until there comes that moment,
just for us, when a set
of free-wheelers waits,
100,000 genes poised
to snatch us
into TIME.

Are they pulled somehow
into the urgency
of sperm swimming toward egg,
the slippery ecstacy
of egg crossing fallopian thresholds
and voila,

  We are just *IN TIME!*

TIME
the sweet hallucination
of our senses
that gives us a home.

The cells of my tongue
forming these poems
were once in another galaxy,
or the nose of a camel
or the blood of an enemy.
We are all over each other
everywhere.

The hemoglobin of Black
turns up in the cornea of Klansman
who when he looks at
burning crosses with his cruel eye
is seeing through the blood
of his Black brother's body.

How graciously our cells,
even the most estranged,
have penetrated compassion
to commune us into a life.

Our nuclei have lived
so much longer
than we, so full of memory
and experience
and the unknown.

Forever everywhere,
all our bodies are gypsies
always ready to pull up tents,
to release back
into the inexhaustible!

This is the moment
    to take a rest
        from infinity!

A Hard Run

I always pitched dead center
across home plate
the summer I was ten.
Frankly, I had a gift.
I was steady, predictable,
reliable as the dust.

You knew when I walked
onto the mound
what was coming next,
I'd give you no surprising
angles or dips,
just a long underhanded arc,
friendly and available.

Everybody got a hit.
When I pitched,
they felt **good**
while I got a rhythm going
so smooth it took maybe
a dozen or so batters
before we got three outs
off of the other team.

Of course, Miss Lathrop
pulled me out by the third inning
and put in Amelia Quickby
who was tricky.
With her, no one hardly
got on base.

Yep, I was history early,
out of play.
But before I left the field,

those kids knew in their green bones
what it felt like to hit
that plump white ball
SMACK at the sky.

I gave them,
more than once,
the long slide into home
and the sweat of a hard run.

Lucky thing—
they can't trade you
in sixth grade.

I've never been so steady since.
Been known to let loose
a wild pitch or two
over the years
if you check the neighborhood.

One thing, though,
I've tried to keep *you*
in my game—
just know, when I'm around,
if I have *anything*
to say about it—

When I see you heading
for Home,
I'll make sure the umpire
flings his arms wide
and cries—
"SAFE."

Basic Hygiene

Ethel Dahir always had dirt
underneath her fingernails
even on Sundays
when we went to her house
for pie made from strawberries
right out of her garden—
and coffee, well, the grown-ups
drank cup after cup
while Ethel squeezed me
lemonade in a tall
blue glass
with clouds of ice.

It was fascinating
how Ethel didn't totally wash up
before our visit—I'd sneak looks
at her strange hands which I supposed
were because Ethel lived in the country
and had married a farmer during
the Depression—*"Absolutely
Salt of the Earth,"*
my Mom would always say
as we drove toward Ethel
and away from town.

Reddish-brown, like good rock,
the backs of Ethel's hands made
the teacup fingers of city ladies
seem pale as slugs.
Dark-blue veins were merging rivers
that fed into her torn knuckles
full of new scratches and tiny scars,
I'd run my eyes along her lined

rough fingers until,
there they were,
her jagged nails and the dirt beneath
which would leave me to wonder
about basic hygiene—and the pie,
like did she really clean the strawberries
or had they gone into the cooking pot
with just a little dirt left on them, too?

I would go home and dream
of Ethel's hands:
how life had gross and fertile secrets
beyond my Mother's house,
and wake up queasy like when
I'd see earthworms' slimy bodies
on the sidewalks after heavy rain.

One Sunday visit
Ethel took me out
to dig potatoes
after a sun-shower.
"Enough of all this chatting,"
she said,
"Now's just the best time
to stick your hand into the earth
and poke around
'til you get a good-sized one,
then loosen it up."

Kneeling,
she took those mysterious
fingers of hers,
worked them into the ground,
wet from rain and warm
just to give me the feel for digging.
I fell to my knees

in my fancy clothes,
with a sudden thirst for the Earth,
plunged in my arms
alongside Ethel,

And in that moment
when she pulled up
out of the dirt,
right then
Ethel's hands flew
into my soul
like the Book of Revelation,

I knew that all summer long,
Ethel wore the Earth
like her Sunday clothes.

The Starwheel

to my mother and father, thank you for this life

Through the dropping darkness, the old farmhouse lists toward us in the snow-spiralling wind, gathering us in its net of light. We ski in short ankle-wobble slides, weary from the tumbling hills and miles we covered along Cedar Creek. Up ahead, the dogs fall sideways into the sweeping drifts, emerging snow-dusty, tired, with a fierce eye for home and a nose for hot gizzard from the New Year's turkey.

Heading home—with our New Year's group of friends through the blown fields of blue-gray light, where the curved dogwood branches are red as burgundy. We ski toward the new year, while the old winks out like lights fading in any solitary country house, leaving the dark new land. Each of us moves in a slow slide of reverie— memories scattering like the filigree of cedar twigs on the snow beneath us.

Two motherless New Years have passed me. I still see the braided backs of my mother's hands during the holidays, grinding pecans, dropping batter from a wet teaspoon on the hot greased pans and later dusting the warm balls with powdered sugar. Mother, your pecans and butter still linger in my mouth, like sweet unspoken thoughts.

I did not understand your life, or mine. Out here, the night air is clear. Your spirit is present in my breathing. If only your own breath could warm this space around

me—cold as untended fires in ice-fishing shacks on the
frozen lake near our Minnesota cottage years ago.
There one December, you, Father and I tested old
Christmas lights and celebrated when they all went on!
Heavy bulbs with peeling green and red paint, the blue
paper "Star of Bethlehem" lit from inside, glowing, and
the silver tinsel that nearly killed our old black three-
legged cat.

My father, your husband: he was on a Willy Loman roll
through who-knows-what state in a turquoise '54 Chevy
selling fire and life insurance to small towns, carrying his
policies and the brown dye for his side burns in his
valise. Didn't want people to think they were buying
from an old man!

But that December, he came off the road and we landed
together on Lake Minnetonka for the holidays. Your
pecan wizardry and the old tree lights strung together all
our whirling Christmases like winter constellations
return each year. On Christmas Eve you would point
them out first on your round Starwheel that rotated for
the seasons. Then we'd go into the night to find them:
Orion, Taurus, the Pleiades, reliable as infinity.

Skiing slowly home, the scents of the past are so strong I
believe I can shake off my skis and return to that
kitchen. Alone with you while you bake, I'll approach
you with questions, questions to release the unspoken:

> "Ma," I will ask: "When somebody you love
> dies, is it like the movies where you're
> together in an amber light holding hands, and
> it's all hushed and you hold the dying person

they smile and fall back on large pillows?"

You look at me funny, startled out of your baking. But I keep on.

> "Or can people die before you get to tell
> everything you want them to know . . . Ma?"

You smudge the old black cat with your powdery white fingers, turning away because you don't like to talk straight on about hard things. So I go after the warm cookies and plug in the Christmas tree lights, not knowing that I've just met eternity—the silence of what I couldn't know you would never know.

An endless echo like the snapping shut of my father's valise in some town after a stranger bought no life insurance.

Slowly skiing into the wash of light across snow outside the farmhouse, I arrive full of speech. But when I walk inside—the house is Robin's house on Cedar Creek, the kitchen smells of fruitcake and cranberries, not pecans. You've gone. Everyone else has shaken the snow from their clothes and pulled off their boots. The dogs have sunk weak-legged to their sleeping spots, already dreaming in moist snorts by the steaming socks on the radiators.

I shake off the unspoken, warm my nose, my hands, and join the celebration. We begin to drink hot red wine together—friends huddled like the Pleiades in the orphan night.

When To Stay Put

Once again, as the long winter night
flings down its storm,
my husband, dog, two cats
are deep in the covers, all soggy fur,
wet snoring, sudden scratching,
vibrating the pillows,
greedy for the quilt,
leaving one slice
of bed small as the new moon
for me to dream in.

When I reach out
for warmth and space,
the dog becomes a whale,
immoveable, slumbering
in her oceanic deep,

While Richard, the sly thief,
has silently fastened the covers tight
to his bed side, leaving me open
to the dark.

So abandoned
by these sleep-robbers
of the night I blast them
with my reading light and write
mad midnight poetry
until Richard lifts our heft
of dog over to the soft place

near his belly. He loses for a moment
his stealthy quilt-grip,

I dive into the cave
of body heat, pulling covers
so tight the cats sail
into the air, dropping down
on our bodies like stone,
no purr
interrupted: cats know
a good thing, *when to stay put*
in the night,

Suddenly the bed opens,
full of promise,
no struggle left,
or poems.

I lie, loose-limbed, listening,
a witness to them all,
each wheeze and sigh a little
prayer of breath,
suddenly struck
by the mysterious
gift of shelter.

Surely Life-Giver
   Bringer of Blessings,
      has stopped to rest
         with us,

Alive,
   inside the purr
      of cat,

Outside—
      the wind's claw.

Homecountry

i.

Let me gather up
the bundles of straw
I have farmed from
your body. Let me
harvest you after all
these years
of full moons.

In the back country of our life,
let me lie in
the hush of
dry, shorn fields
in this autumn light
full of praise for you
who anchor me
like the backyard's great oak
split open by storms
where just now
in the deep hollow
of its trunk
the untamed cat hides
her new-born kittens.

Be careful!

Don't pry too much
into her safe dark spot
or she'll carry them off
just as too close a look
will scare away
the secrets that protect
our bliss.

ii.
Just as I lie back
in the easy chair
of your returns,
all comfy,

Just when I feel dug
into the dirt and mud of you,
all your perennials reliable,
steady, year by year,

You turn into
a driving rain,
mix up all the bulbs
and metaphors
ransacking the garden.

Earth is murk again,
oozing where I step,
in pools of water
that gather
in the uneven ground.

Once again
I take up the hoe,
dig into myself
again,
often brought to my knees
to fertilize,
wildly, savagely
I compost,
for awhile just dirt, bones,
rags, seed and stone,
old vegetables from
other seasons.

No one knows me,
a fierce mulch,
beyond friends and home,
until I drive down
to the surprising
choir of earthworms
singing just for me.

In that moment,
I look up.

There you are,
at the backdoor,
looking very much like
someone I used to know.

Leaping up
wildly in love
with myself,
honorably self-reliant,
immensely cultivated,

I still long
for you
there in the doorway,
forever new.

This Moon Is Not Cool

This moon is not cool,
she's a bright-hot coal
in the indigo ash
of late summer sky,
burning red
and full.

As far away
as this fire
in the night,
you are,
my lover,

I am an Indian
driven from the wilderness
of your belly
into the cities
where I look up
to find the stars.

There are
no celestial bodies.

Night is simply a dirty face
with no caress,

Only now
this moon
burning red and hungry
fills up
with your fire,

Down here
on Longing Street
I am in flames,

Where only the aloof
street lamps
burn with me.

This Is What Women Know

Poets go about stealing poems
in public,
so here at the cafe,
I'm ready to ambush this couple,
passionately eavesdrop
on their shared life,

but don't go too close! Be respectful.

Just a glimpse!

These two, women together,
companions,
are quite old.

Old enough to be with each other
since the First World War,
older maybe than Rip Van Winkel
after his long sleep.

They linger together.

The hair of one is so thin-white,
her scalp shows pink and naked.

The other woman's fingers shake
as she lifts her cup.

I imagine way back when:
her hand, with a different trembling,
touches her partner, there,
at the soft back of her head
where she remembers suddenly—

like heat lightning—
remembers when her hair was
startling-thick, black.

This couple has been
together so long
while one speaks,
the other stares off into the distance
yet drifts back in
at just the correct moment
like the right dream pierces sleep,
and answering,
she calls her life companion,

   "Grace."

So I learn her name,
and, like the gift that sometimes
comes to poets lying in wait,
"Grace" is just the right name
for what is unfolding before me
in a fairy tale, long over-due,
that must be written
to join the sleeping Snow White—

This is their story:
How to stay awake to beauty,
touch Old Love's hair,
and listen,
when we are ancient
with so much to say
and ripe as a teenager.

This is what women know.

The Kiss

i.

Just after
the intermingling
breath
come those naked
dampnesses:
the lips
moving closer
like continental drift
until
all cells within our
expectant bodies
shift
their permeable
boundaries
while
two
solitary
mouths
meet with the intimacy
of nose.

Ear lobes and nostrils
awaken
to each other's
tendernesses,
the languorous
tongue
amidst teeth's
miniature
nips

stirs us
to underwater sounds
of primordial journeys.

We sink back
to THE BEGINNING
when all life was

ooze and warmth
and One
our throats yield
again and again
to this ancient mingling
saliva
breath
flesh
while the uvula
hangs down
in dark rapture

witnessing everything.

ii.

When you
are lonely

or this world
seems too
rotten
even for
the compost heap

go lie
on the earth—

Kiss her.

Go to the water—

Listen.

These are bodies
who respond
to your loneliness,

the earth
and waters
can be melancholy, too,
like the sound
of birds
flying
into extinction.

Do you hear
how they need you?

Go.

Do you feel
the wounded air
tremble

for your embrace?

The Body of Belonging

*"Like anybody, I would like to live a long life,
longevity has its place. When I die, give me a big
funeral. Say that I tried to love somebody. I tried
to walk the walkway. Say that I wanted to leave
behind a committed life, then my living will not
be in vain."*
Dr. Martin Luther King, Jr.

i.

When thunder
speaks your name so loud
it brings you here,
sets you down
to begin your walk
on this Earth,
time passes,
hardship and beauty
write themselves on your body,

When you are loosened from childhood
to climb the tree of impossible choice,
then, in this one life,
may you create a dream
　beyond what breaks you,
　　　beyond the ruined fruit,
the shocking loss,

Beyond betrayals,
　　or poor esteem,
most definitely,
may you always dream

beyond your *"failure,"*
or even what you deserve
because the path to
"Where you ought to be
by this time in life"
is paved with shadows.

No one necessarily makes it.
Fresh air has not
reached its potential,
rainforests are not fulfilled,
the brass ring has slipped
the grasp of the oceans,
photosynthesis is underemployed,
and the atmosphere
is seeking welfare.

Even the sky is broken,
hangs its head,
the stars tremble,
which has provoked the Milky Way
to lose its grip, crying out
to the sky,
  "Don't give up, we belong
    together and we need you,"
so sky lifts up
beyond its damages,
digs deep
  for faith
    to back up the stars.

And if we've "made it"

we've none of us
done so
alone, on our own,
even with hard work
and the courageous
pull on the bootstrap,
we're each of us standing
on the shoulders
of all the Freedom movements
of history, standing on our class,
privileges, inheritance, entitlements,
so put a loop in your success
and throw that rope
over the fence
to those still back here,

cast on to the body
of belonging.

The deepest bond
 is the dream that carries you
  beyond anyone's luck,
   even your own,
    beyond anyone's control,
     or deception,
      joining you
       with all the other dreamers
       until death do us part:
        this is the true marriage.

ii.
About pain:

even though you *deserve* to feel
only your own pain
and degradation
for all this life-time,
even though
you have *earned*
the most bitter revenge
against the ugliest acts,
nevertheless, we beg you
in love and admiration,
be merciful to yourself,
please!
          Imagine that you can
release yourself from these injuries
just enough to jump from the wheel,
all your wounds in flames,
into the arms of
the rest of us out here
because we are dying for your company:
     all we can do is share
        the medicine
          of fire—
               Use the heat.

A Few Minutes From Now

Imagine how
fast
death comes
and goes,
in this moment
we gather
to celebrate poetry
and the earth,
our ceremony
of song and belief,

the death of every tree
    that will be felled
        this next hour,

        the immense hillside
            burned to a running wound
                of red clay
                    in this hour,

        the child who will
            catch the bullet
            a few minutes
            from now,

Oh, imagine the many
    bodies of poems
        that will go down
            with them,

        the poems that might

have rested,
like Buddha,
   beneath those great trees
   and become enlightened,

the poem denuded
  and clear cut
   of its vowels
   of praise
    for the slain hillside's
    meadows and bees,

the poem that bleeds
  from the dying kid's
   fading heart
   to become
    a stain in the street.

In our lifetime,
  any hour everywhere
   must include a funeral
   that registers
   so much passing.

What is the velocity
  of extinction,

   while every poem
   nourished by nature
   is at risk
    from all this loss,
    mourning so many
    loved ones.

Like songbirds
who seek a tree
to light in
that is not marked
for death,
poems must fly
longer and longer
distances
through the
failing air.

For Angela. Who Is Beyond

for poet sister and mentor, Angela Peckenpaugh,
Memorial Reading, Woodland Patterns, Milwaukee
October 5, 1997

Angela,
the way I see it,
some people
are simply stars.
Not just a single glowing light body,
but an entire
constellation
our community looks up to
and says, *"Yes,*
there she is in the Wisconsin sky-
the mysterious Angela Formation"
which if you look carefully
on a clear evening
appears very much a woman
sitting intent over a desk
that words spill from,
streaking across the night
to pick up other starstuff
by the hand
as they pass.

You may seem far away,
Angela,
but we hold you fixed
in our vision,
pull you back
with the scope of our imagination,
love, in gratitude,
in touch.

Down here
our little piece of Earth
is emptier now,
our fire has lost power.

The bee is travelling
with less pollen
to the flower.

But with you out there,
Beyond,
eternity has a lot more quality,
seems closer, more friendly,
dusted, as it is,
with your luster,
gilded forever,
with your spark.

You Can Reach For Me

*with thanks to my Aunt Jetti and Uncle Lou
who taught me about "lucky stones"
on Nantucket Island*

You can reach for me this summer
like a stone full of blessing
surrounded by
a white circle
complete with no breaks,
for luck.
I am that steady.
I lie in the shade collecting shadows
all day, the moon all night.

Never say a stone is dead.

You can pick me up
in your humid palm
to feel cool enduring promise
in the seed of your body.

Who we are for each other
in this season
of hardship,
this yielding of summer,
who we are for each other
can happen only
if you reach out for me,
then I'll slip
into your hands.

In the Neighborhood

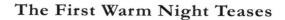

The First Warm Night Teases

Spring's shadow-tinted fog,
roused from the drowsy river,
sneaks down its windows
   like a stretch limo
    taking a risk,
fresh air's
  a romance language
   in love
    with moist beginnings,
     such a tease,
until earth
  loosens up,
   and the light
    returns,
     rolls away the stone
     to release hopes
     that perished
      in winter's hard attitude,
fresh green shoots press through
  good dirt directly into
   your gospel heart until
    the choir hits the high note!

Spring doesn't come the same way
for everyone,
but some things never change,
winter stars spill off
  the starwheel onto
   the hard-top reservoir
   above our block
   scattering

like tossed bottle glass.
Harley riders Butch and Jason
journey up to the hilltop,
after closing time at
"The Alley-Cat Tap"
to check out an easier sky
beyond the copper street lights,
they look down to see
the hard concrete cover gleam
its toughness back at them—
    then they take their bottles
from paper bags, finish them off,
with a shout, throw hard,
arm muscles wail,
hard so the glass shatters, each piece
wild with their power. They slap
each other's back, whack
against cool leather of their jackets,
shake hands over their first night of Spring
while early dawn comes on,
along the wire fences
and pale stone walls
freeing up its gold
like Rapunzel's hair.

Down below, on our block,
all the winter refuse releases
from under the snow cover,
blending its smells. Some days,
the whole street looks like one
huge waste they can just cart away—
except for the cats on their backs
arching along naked sidewalks

in sun patches,
or a whole garden
of pastel plastic geraniums planted
in neat rows on the corner
by the abandoned tavern—
used to be *"Marcella's 5th Avenue."*

Soon the first Iris will wave
their loose, open bodies like floozies,
swaying to the church bells of St. Casimirs
after months when the winter streets
slept with one eye open . . .
stretched out, silent.

Now kids wake them up with games—
*"Hey, Delmar, it's you and me against
Jose and Charlie . . ."*
they toss the ball back and forth
over the heads
of the nuts-and-lugbolt Uncles
and Pops fixing Chevies and pick-ups,
the boom boxes run alongside
with the latest tunes,
around corners into the brick-rough
cigarette-butt, hoop-full alleys,
everyone ready to hit the deck before
Butch, Jason, Tony and Bill ride on by,
their motorcycles hot to the touch;
you've got to slide your car
easy, practicing with your brakes
for the tight squeeze of summer.

Our houses shift even closer
in the yielding mud,

lean into an unwanted kiss,
window screens put an end
to privacies
and quiet,
we're close as brussel sprouts.

Neighbor dog's out wailing again,
abandoned early morning high on
the second-story porch, behind the trees
just like last fall. Except they got
a young spring Doberman
to keep it company--
pup's only up to a whimper.
But soon they'll mourn together full-tilt
on their ledge of neglect
keening for hours through the trees
until the leaves howl.

Winter is pacing,
pacing the hard fenced-up
reservoir like a wiry old big-city
boxer looks for a jumping-off place,
coaching Spring to sprout from
his toughened heart
into tulips who flaunt
their ripe, gaudy petals,
daffodils raise their sun-faces
to witness the mornings
along with bundles of babies
budding on the clustered front porches,
their new bodies
such soft ears
listening for Spring,

until the old Fighter relents,
saunters down to us,
trailing bottle glass, and star cinders,
worn-out from the wind chills,
ready to ease up
and bloom
on our block
for another round.

We Closed His Yellow Eyes

When the city broke him with its wheels
and he dragged home, half his body dangling,
still purring—dying, when he stared past us
so hard all the vacant back yards this side
of town were in his eyes, we sent him
out to sea: our small black cat, "*Mellow*,"

who, when you swooped him in your arms,
spread out his paws for a wide embrace,
ready to sleep in the curve of your neck
forever. Nothing ruffled him,
except the street, so he'd make his stand
to come back in, how he would howl
on the front porch, like his life
depended on it, after we'd pushed
him out along with Lucky who, even with
no claws, tackled the alleys and the raw nights
until even the neighbors knew Lucky was
King of the block, facing down all contenders,
arriving home in the morning, ready
to sleep, both ears intact, with ghosts of birds,
mice and vanquished tom cats in his eyes
while Mellow knew better than us,
all cats aren't alike.

He lacked the city's edge.

First we laid him in a cardboard box
and carried him far away to Cedar Creek.
At its most flooded point we dug,
throwing the pick axe hard into the ground
to put him in—deep. The digging went slow.

Long shadows of fence slats fell onto us,
creek waters streaming by, while the box
stood near, ready. "Not yet," we said.
"Got to go deeper so the animals won't get him."

At last we took him from the box and laid him
in the hole on dried grasses to soften
the bed. We closed his yellow eyes.
When we threw dirt lightly on him it felt
like thunder. Later in a strong wind, we burned
his box in the field, standing in the heat until
ashes blew toward the creek. That was the last.
Odd together, flooded waters and ashes:
the rush of water, and the end of fire—
both elements lap at you, both have tongues.
But ashes end the fire; water goes on and on.

Close by, currents that flooded all the way
to the wheat field were streaming back down
to lower ground, flowing down to the rivers,
and finally to the sea, dying back, breaking,
rushing up on the sand, rushing, rushing
away from streets with no mercy
out to the swelling sea.

Turtle Alley

Mizheekay,
  a huge snapper wanders
into our alley,
   old spirit,
       dry shell,
miles from the river.
The alley kids who
hang out at Joan's place
turn it over,
watch it scramble
to right itself,
they turn it over
again.

"Don't let it bite you, man,"
a bunch of them, stoned,
young, pick it up,
its feet and tail waving.
"Those suckers
can be mean,"
turtle flies
in their hands.

"Hey," Jimmie says,
"Let's take it inside,
get it high,
then turn it over,
man, it will really
flip out!"

Joan grabs the turtle away

into the house,
her two small boys,
Jess and Joe,
and all the alley kids
disappear with her,
soon there's the party
her latest boyfriend, B. J., throws,
who's so sick now
they call him "Bone,"
still he parties hard all night,
burning his last light
in the tiny attic: Joan,
her boys, the alley kids,
and somewhere indoors,
Mizheekay,
the old snapper.

Not too much later
we go over,
tap on Joan's door,
go in past Rag, the matted
long-hair tom cat,
go up to the attic,
band is keyed up, nasty,
Joan is flying so fast
her little kids have a contact high.

I shout: *"Where's the turtle,
Joan, I know a place for it."*

She looks suspicious,
plus she thinks we owe her because
her boyfriend, B. J., he has silicosis
in his lungs, but even so, one night

when our cat, Mellow, got stuck
on the roof and wailed like a coyote,
B. J. climbed up the ladder while
Joan held onto his oxygen tank below,
B. J. had to make the rescue as one
of his last acts of manhood,
his lungs laboring like inmates
doing hard time,
he brought Mellow down,
so Joan, she does nothing
for free,
thinks we owe her,
and now she owns the turtle.

"*Yeah, where ya gonna take it?*"
she yells, sneering over the music.

I lie: "*A friend's got a creek for it.*"

She looks at me hard,
her eyes saying,
"I got enough to take care of
without some damn turtle,"

Then shrugs, "*It's in the bathtub,*"

The kids shout,
"*But it's ours, Ma,*"
she raises her hand, fast,
they flinch and shut up.

"You don't own nothing,
You kids want that snapper,
you gotta pay me rent for it."

Downstairs
in the tub,
circling in shallow water
with fuzz and old hair,
slipping up the slick sides
blinded by porcelain,
we find
the old snapper.

Old relative,

You pull in your head
and feet,
trust nobody,
leaving behind only your shell,
with its curved,
hopeful beauty
of ancient, perfect etchings,

we gather you up,
    cut through backyards
        to release you
            into the river's
                tires and muddy currents,

where still you can
    smell freedom,
        stretch out your whole body
            to leap away from us
                fast.

Old protector
   adrift
      in turtle alley.

"Mizheekay": Ojibwe word for "turtle." In some Native American traditions, North America is called "Turtle Island" and pictures show a huge sacred turtle carrying Earth on its back.

The Near Miss

Breasts straight out like commands,
carrying a stick-bat,
brassy tough, she walks
in the middle of the street—
she owns it.

You drive around the corner,
ball game's breaking up,
kids gleam in your headlights,
you slam your brakes, fast,
when she looms suddenly
in your windshield,
big, like an outdoor movie,
lipstick ripe, blond,
the neighborhood queen,
bad-mouthed siren,
great legs—lean, muscled—young.

She loves to invite the close calls,
the near miss. She will never die,
always be young, forever cool,
"*Hey, watch it . . . man,*" she says,
real low,
right into your open window.

Her friends toss the ball
back and forth across the street,
for one mean instant you figure
you could pick them off
like bottles on a fence and be
covered by insurance.

But you slide along, windows open,
real slow; she teases your fenders,
bat on her shoulder, ivory arms
shine in the headlights,
sweat on her face and neck.

It's hot: summer night on Bremen street,
and hey, you want
your street life back,
don't you, your early,
easy glamour,
you and your car and your duties
are the only game you play now,
you want to get out
and kiss her
until all her boldness
fires you up
so you can belong to the heat
again.

Windows
wide open,
trying to get more air,
you slide along,
real slow.

Clarke Street Moon

This moon over Clarke St.
  is one sliver of cold steel
    riding the sky.
Stars—just ice fragments
scattered in the huge night vault.
Wind's a laser, chilling streets
into an asphalt galaxy.

Been like this for a week.

Lots of dead batteries—
  "*Alley Cat Tap*" is the only
    hot spark on our block.
Got a good box that pulls you
off the street, maybe Dizzy Gillespie
on "Night in Tunisia," or some
saxaphone with a ruby tongue.
"*The Alley Cat*"—barstool thighs,
brandy shots, beer, smoke—and talk.
Seems like Joey Simone's
always behind the bar.
And that slack faced ex-athlete,
Hank, or is it Chuck,
is leaning in,
    close to Joey, chatty:
how they tore down the goal post
in '43 after his 88 yard run,
and his girl was a cheerleader—
what a catch—
        in little white socks.

Joey never says too much.
But he doesn't back off either.

Round the bend in the bar,
deep in the corner, there's Helen—
laid off last month. She slips over
to play the juke box, sits with
a marguerita flush and salty lips,
light from the neon Schlitz clock
  with Mt. Everest background
    plays off her face.

She never says too much
and backs off all the time.

It's been a run of cold nights.

Even Cliff's silver 750 BMW is frozen
to the curb out front—won't crank up.
So back in he comes,
      tears off his helmet,
        red-faced,
          beating together his hands—
    "Gimme a brandy!"

At last the hot jazz,
quick shots and Joey Simone
begin to vaporize all troubles
and chill factors
into a warm, steady mist
  forming on the windows,
    leaks slowly outside

into the mean midwestern night
to freeze on the back steps,
garbage cans and cat whiskers
of our block on Clarke St.

Winter Solstice, Corner of Twilight and North

Do you see, tonight, how the snow is falling, falling over our town, so apparently peaceful, summoned somewhere from out of the distressed sky, the snow flies, over the city. The snow, so white, white as the once pure mother's milk of Christmas past, light and dusty as cocaine, it falls, gilding the city with its sleep, its relief, while the spiked Star in the East is shining, shining, too, on our shimmering and huddled homeless, even on the street corners there is no room, all the alleys are mangers, and some unfathomable somewhere wise men are at the crossroads, seeking direction, aren't they?

Yes, truly, deeply, now, this is the season to pray, to search, to recall magic, to beg for mercy. Some people among us are so tired of the cold, can you feel how they just begin to sink to their knees, O, it would feel so good to rest. But then the enduring Wind of the North comes to them in voices and urges, "You *must keep your eyes open, you must stay awake. It is not time for you to give up, even though you are crawling.*"

This somebody to whom the wind has called out, responds—"*I'm tired. There is too much ice—even the blood running in the streets has gone cold, and forgotten. I just can not turn the corner on all this pain, this loss, this death. Face it, it's a nasty world. The sky is a nightmare of vicious stars. Even the buds inside the frozen branches cannot face another spring. It is the worst of times.*"

And the North Wind says, *"Not yet, not yet, do not give up, I am at your back, I will help you."*

"No," you say, *"I am down. We are all down. For the count. There is not enough love, not enough hope to save me."*

The North Wind pauses, for once, *"O. K. I hear you. So, since you are down, down on your knees and weeping, it is good. Use it. Stay there, and you just pray, pray for us all. Go all the way to the bottom. We need you."*

You say, *"You mean, all I have to do is to cry out my suffering, call out our pain?"*

"You're on to something," said the North Wind, moved by the magnitude of this grief. *"My friend—even the elements, yes, all of us need someone to just fall down and let loose all the sorrows! Let their sound lift up your voice. Make your prayers wail with the revealing dark, and resound full of the earth's needs. I will take your bitter cries and your tears, I, the wind, will blow them clear and crisp, I will wrap them in my wings of strong and burnished air!"* The North Wind shook with inspiration.

"Now, you see that lonely group of humans over there who have come out in the longest night? I will carry your prayers to them in all their longing, I will enter them as poems do, or grace, like a miraculous intervention of soul, and light the wick of their heart. So they can celebrate, even now!"

You say, *"But still I cannot believe. Can there be anything unknown, or unseen beyond this stupid, bitter world? And anyway, so what? It's just foolish myths, smoke and mirrors! We are doomed."*

"All that I ask," said the Wind, *"is that you do not suffer in silence! You think you are alone. I understand this. But your despair is not wasted, the Earth hears you! So even on your knees, know even in the moment you surrender hope and cry out, even when you want just to sleep and to forget, and the snow is falling, beckoning to you - I ask only one thing. **Remember—the first move in magic is to call out.** Then you wait. You listen. Maybe for a long long while you wait, while the snow falls and falls."*

"And then?" You ask.

"Be on the look-out, for just maybe there will be a shift, a little lift, some of your sorrows, your desolation will catch the wind's back and fly out over the town, perch atop the melancholy street lights, and rejoice—anyway."

"Nope," you say, *"Just can't do it. Not gonna be on the look-out, staring up in space for mysteries, or grace. You'll find me looking down. Still on my knees."*

The North Wind, preparing for take off in the transfiguring cold, says: *"O.K., like I said, I'm with you. Let's start there."*

Espresso

This liquid ecstasy
pulls your body to freedom
like a freight train express
in a dark tunnel
bursts into the night
with full moon overhead
pouring cream
and white gold
over the land
so light and darkness
are lovers inside you.

This wild nectar
you ride everyday
towards madness,
second shift
or God
spikes your rhythm
makes your heart surge
sacred, dark
as the Black Madonna
and as full of soul.

Live! At the Jazz Estate

January 1993

Deep inside, in the nightclub light,
the Estate brings you this gift,
world-class—count on it,
right here in Cream City,
his name is Spike Robinson and right now
Spike's tenor is heavy fog
smoking through curved brass.
Mercy! Mercy has brought some heat to this old
blighted world this nasty January where the sun has
covered its face. Dusky glass over cool Miles Davis'
photo on the back wall catches Spike's profile—do you
see how the breath beats in his temple as he blows?
"Either it's love or it isn't" is the tune.
Spike is reaching for that long creamy high note
before he takes the solo home,
the drummer clicks along behind him like a train
heading for the station.
Can you feel it?
Then Spike hangs his tenor on his shoulder
while the man at the piano
takes over the solo track.

The night is breathing hard
as a love poem longing to happen.
Spike reaches, yes, reaches this time
for his cigarette that's been waiting for him burning
for him next to his lukewarm beer,
takes a long drag,
his horn sways on his shoulder
a languorous snake charmed by the piano man
who is working his way around the changes.

The night starts to cook—*Spike Robinson is smokin'!*
All there is
is the music.

Just now you forget that outside this room
half the world is crawling on its knees,
you leave behind your troubles, your losses,
you check the blood streaming down
the face of the earth at the door.

Briefly you forget that Miles beat women.
You forget that cigarettes kill.
You lean over to the guy next to you
who has just let a riff perfect and smooth
bring a "yeah" deep out of him,
you say, *"Hey, Dick, could I bum a cigarette—make it
two cigarettes?"* He gives you Chesterfields,
no filters, and you don't even smoke
except tonight you're smokin' with Spike
and you give the other to the someone beside you
who's your beloved dearly, your turbulent other,
your significant nobody or maybe, simply,
your own true self who earlier you were lost with in
the homey JUST EVERYDAY ANY NIGHT
and this morning, hey,
didn't you run out of toilet paper
and tonight you snatched dinner together
so fast it was illegal
like stealing lipstick from dimestores
and **wham** the 10,000th dinner hour,
or dinner moment you shared together was over
and, *tell the truth now,*
didn't the cold night measure ahead of you like
a school kid's ruler—12 exact familiar inches
tunnelling into the future with its steady little
arithmetic toward the 10 O'clock news, except some

fine soul across town calls suddenly: *"Do you know
Spike Robinson is playing 'The Estate' tonight?"*
and the door to Heaven swings open.

You look up.
You look at each other with that look
that was in your first look,
the look that binds,
the recognition that God has just walked in
on eighth notes
and the winter night
which wore such plain clothes,
garments so tried and true,
the night is indeed still young, so here you are,
in the nightclub delight, you hand over that
Chesterfield to your lover, who flicks you a light,
you fire up those stolen moments,
the forbidden smoke slides into the soul
of your lungs who forgive you instantly and

"You won't see me cryin' anymore"
is the nice old tune.
Such sweet moments,
you don't watch your back.
Nothing is happening anywhere else in the world.
You are in the state of grace. And when all the tunes
come home, the wee small hours are through,
you will go back through that door,
back out to the city of confusion,
your pulse is high, a praise song,
you walk out right into the paralyzed eyes
of the wounded world,
raise up your hands and testify:
*"Get up, get up, **RISE** . . . Life is a wind instrument,
so stand up and blow."*

The Blues Train

With a tired intimacy, we prepare to go out, and I notice
James reach to turn off the light. I wonder, will there be
one more time that I see exactly that gesture—the dark
hair on his arm, the veins rising under his pale skin.
Hard work has made the flesh tight over his wrists, the
muscles of his forearm work when he flips the switch.
Sometimes isn't it the unbearable detail that keeps you
coming back?

Since it's almost the end of the year, we've been holding
out for Christmas Eve, the impossible holiday
performance. We're going down the street, to the bar at
Century Hall, to hear Julia Dale play the blues. Blues
for Christmas, to tie it all up with a blue ribbon. Just
like Rosemary Clooney and Bing. The night is very cold,
and we are numb. There is no snow, and the dark
stretch from Belleview to the parking lot across from the
Hall is quiet, windless. No cars. Everyone is already
where they belong.

I always love coming up to the Hall along Farwell, its
huge front windows emerge, glowing in the dark wood
panels. You feel like some immense antique magic ship
has sailed up and moored in this strange old world, just
for you. But then the angles of James' face cut the night
in the lamplight. Can I go on, into the familiar bar
where we have been so many times. Tonight, every
drink will measure out the loss, inching toward the wide
open mouth of the New Year.

Unaware, James goes on in, ahead of me. The front

hallway is bare, without heat, so it's a relief to move into the main room with its rich hues of wood, the large bright windows of the kitchen, and an immense long-needled Christmas tree reaching towards the high ceiling. The room is so full of bustle and hope, even the tree is singing, *"Hallelujah, Baby."* Yet all this promise hurts. My romance fading, turned into a series of one night stands, like the old year, winking out its last lights. I need a brandy, sweet and hot on my throat. And Julia's blues.

Somehow when she plays, she touches the sore, lonely spots of life, eases them out into the open and invites you along. Along on the blues train, "Come on, come on, come on, catch the blues train," she half sings, half talks. With my spoiled love dragging on me I wonder how it might feel to have a piano as a steady lover.

Actually, Julia is very local, like a side street. Her theme song, known only between Belleview and North is the "Hot Applesauce Blues." "Blues, key of C," she would call out, about juicy hopes and ice cold lovers. Yes, she moves along the inside track. Really very local, but I've got an icy lover, and she has a little something. Century Hall is good for the inside track, and folks who fall through the cracks, well, the Hall's there to catch them like a sturdy angel.

I need to find Julia, look into the large barroom towards the grand piano where the sleek wooden bartop curves into a corner. Not many bars have grand pianos. Not many bars have that kind of faith. Julia's there, taking a break, apparently, or maybe just waiting to begin.

Waiting for the night to get ready. She's wearing her old-fashioned black velvet dress—the velvet has a shine to it from wear at the seams, and at the back from late night hours on the piano bench; pearl earrings with rhinestones, large, that dangle whenever she moves her head, like flashes of moonlight in the murky light of the bar. Julia's hard to get at. From a distance, she appears very young. Closer you see the darkness under the eyes, the shallow, muddied pools of history, and her face takes on wear. She's small. Her hands—small, seem to get cold easily so she usually has a cup of hot coffee on the end of the keyboard. Between songs, she sits with her fingers cupped for warmth. Doesn't seek anyone out but talks to you if you happen by. I wonder how she feels. Like now, between sets, she seems suspended, the space between the notes.

I've been watching her a lot these past months while James and I turned slowly into a series of one night stands. So I always like to hear her song, *"On The Road."* *"I only sing in bars,"* she'd begin, *"To veterans of small-time wars."* Well, Julia, I'm one of your small-timers, play for me. Now as far as I can tell, Julia never actually goes on the road, she seems the type who doesn't have to go far to get someplace. On the road straight to the heart. Like I said, very local. Yet really, what do I know about her—she usually talks between tunes, not much personal but I could figure some things. She makes a bit of money from her music—all she really likes to do is sit in a corner of a bar and play. Performances put her off, she said. Once she'd opened for John Hammond, Jr. at the Hall with 15 milligrams of valium, sun glasses from Oriental Drugs, and a mauve

hat "for support." Her boyfriend doesn't come around
much. One time I saw him back her into a corner,
pushing at her with his voice, "Why should I hang
around here while you sing about fucking—with all
these men who don't even know you getting turned on."
Guess he can't deal with a woman in her own groove.
After he stalked out, she smoked the next set like it was
an unfiltered camel, you could tell she was bound to
answer something inside herself bigger than that fool.
That's what I'm here for.

Julia's definitely got James' respect, but he isn't wild
about her. I know she touches his tender spots—his
body gets very still. I can feel it. "Oh, she's good on the
keyboard," he'd say, "But she does too much of her own
stuff. I mean, it's not John Lee Hooker, you know —
the real thing."

I wonder does she feel like the real thing? How does
she cope with the night, full of strange people who
aren't used to the Hall or to her. Lonely men, not from
the neighborhood, already drunk at 9:30. People
standing around, waiting, one man weaving so hard he
nearly topples into the bell of the grand piano.
Bartender has to throw himself onto the bar, reach over
and grab him back, just before he hits the strings. I
want to stand behind her when she first sits down at the
keyboard, to share that feeling of beginning, when she
has to pick up the dead weight of the crowd. I wonder,
does she feel on call like I do? Do the piano keys grin at
her like a full set of teeth, hungry, full of longing?

James throws his jacket across a table with the

enthusiasm of dry ice. "I suppose you want to sit near the piano," he murmurs. Goes to get the drinks. But I'm not listening. I look around—can't believe it. No one I know is here, all strange people. But I should realize. Who goes to a bar on Christmas Eve? Not people with families or obligations. Even *The Bugle* advertised Julia's gig: *"Feeling down 'n out on Christmas Eve? Let Julia Dale trim your Christmas tree."*

I feel outside, way outside, like C flat in a demented chord is the way Julia might put it. The Spanish have a special name for such lonely people out on Christmas Eve: *"Los Degraciandos"*— *"those from whom grace has been withdrawn."* I'm lost. I look over behind the bar, and there's Sam Divine, he gives me the high sign and the light glances off the glass he raises so he shines out like some gracious chandelier piercing the fog of the barroom, backlit by all the bottles of whiskey, Metoxa, the dark ales and the light beers. Found—Sam, the fixture that makes you feel at home. Tonight, Century Hall, and Sam Divine, they're the only grace a few of us can call on. Like the blues, you send out the call, they're listening—they respond. All you've got to give back is gratitude.

James sits, simply, no words, yet he is aware of me, this way he has of being almost present, then just as we are about to connect, somehow, vanishing. The Bermuda Triangle has nothing on him. He's in a fitted cotton shirt—Italian, with a pattern of deep reds and blue. He looks lean and remote. His hands seem very big. I wish Julia would come on back and play. Take me away.

Come on, come on, come on, bring those blues.

Finally she moves toward the piano. Usually she puts a bright colored shawl on the hardwood bench, I notice it's there now and for a special touch, she's got a burnished walnut candleholder on the piano, with a round red candle that glows warm and promising.

She begins the set with a rendition of her trademark, "Applesauce Blues." God, Julia—dare to warm up Christmas Eve with "I'll make warm applesauce for you, Baby." Already, I feel better. Maybe the Applesauce Blues is a little tired, but it still hits the spot, she's going to stir up the sweetness, play with you. "Let me put some applesauce in your loving cup." Yes, very local. Brandy's tasting so good, come on, Julia.

Then she fools me, becomes Santa Julia, wholesome, plays "White Christmas" with a jazzy feel, and strange chord progressions tossed in every so often so you don't get lazy, then comes her own version of "The Owl and the Pussycat" that just does me in, it's so sweet and melancholy, ready as I'd been to sail off with James to the land where the Bong tree grows. Wally Wonder who owns a bar on the South-side gets so happy he strides right up to the piano, sits down and plays his old time tunes for 20 minutes while off to the side his wife beats time with her hankie. I hear her say how nice it is to see Wally relax and open up, being at someone else's bar on Christmas Eve. Everybody loves it.

For awhile, Julia seems relieved of Christmas duty. But I'm still waiting. I'm waiting, for something, some change. *Come on, come on,* I remember Julia saying how according to Ellington, blues were built on fractured romances. So come on, Julia, take this broken lover on through to the other side. I remember her saying how according to Ellington, it was O. K. to steal, as long as you steal from yourself. But I'm here to steal a little heat from the Hall, a little fever from Julia, a woman playing the edge, a little fire to get me through, with James so close, so cool. Each gesture, his hands, are so separate. Come on, Julia, get to me, get to me.

Then she's on duty, on call with the blues, teasing the blues, reaching for a groove, suddenly finally I'm caught up rhyming, the blues train yearning, turning round the bend, yes, blues train coming for me, ready to take me away, and suddenly I know I can break for it, leave James close to me as blood, cool James lying in the dust, blues train turning round the bend, making a stop just for me, I can hear Julia, "Oh, you're so cold, baby, you think you can make love alone." But I'm making tracks with the blues train. I'm up, I'm moving, I'm out of the bar. *Hallelujah, Baby.*

I'm gone.

Belonging to the Body

Lust

If I were a writer
of well-groomed habit,
and high discipline,
like May Sarton, perhaps,
I'd just get up
everyday at 5:30 A. M.,
hit the typewriter for three hours,
after a tiny breakfast
of teacakes and honey,
making time like fine jockies
handle an elegant race horse,
a clean well-tuned ride
without sacrificing passion
or depth, with sonnets and chapters
racked up by lunch.

But poems take me
in seizures
that strike
during the insomniacal night
when lines, titles,
terrible troubles,
bits of news,
scenes from old movies
shoot at my feet
like outlaws
who stink of hide-outs
and have no manners.

Daytimes they kidnap me
for hours,

let me love no one else,
drug me so I walk
in a day-dream
so changed
my family cards me at bed-time
like some risky character
who may disturb their establishment.

My journals *hate* exercise.

They want me indoors
pressed in my seat
for hours of immobility,
allowing no food but muffins
and coffee so strong
it quotes the Old Testament
until Jehovah steams into my blood
so I sit sit sit and burn,
spewing out phrases and ugly verbs
against the state of things.

They appreciate when I am in a mess
with lovers or friends so they
can mull over all the murky
details and inside info,
or even better
they love me melancholy,
in moods, stirrings,
and stewing no one will ever
be allowed to read except
a grave-robber because, believe me,
these journals are going with me
when I die.

Can you guess what satisfies them most?

When I spend days,
Hell, years,
picking over titles,
assessing lines
and word choices
for slight shifts
of rhythm or sound
in frequencies possibly only dogs
or rare-eared birds might hear
— or care about —
my journals are fulfilled.

Quivering for the erotic moments
my pilot precise rolling pen
touches down to scratch out a line,
reread, and scratch it in again,

they are against poems
who unfold smoothly
to their true shape,
slip their grasp
and move quickly
into the world,
delighting in the possibility
that each work
could remain open to change
or doubt
for my entire life-time.

They have no conscience,
these journals, only lust
to stuff themselves
with me, me,
they want me driven, and
convinced of the terrible importance
of my own self.

I must record,
and reveal, and revise,
and reveal.

Only then, they lean back
and gloat. I have satisfied
their bodies.

Late In the Season

Me and Vi, we try to tell our friend Edna—
who thinks she's so old and worthless,
we say, *"There's only one Edna,"*
she poo-poos us, says she's past her time,
no use to anybody, says *"Maybe,*
I'll just walk into the creek
'til my hat floats,"
says she can't
get on her knees anymore
to get after the weeds,
"I'm nothing but an old bone
tossed out for the earth to chew on,"
    but we say different, tell her
      she's surprising as a bell pepper
        that's gone past green
          and stands out like a red heart,
            loving her like we do,
              we wonder how can we
                make her *feel* it?

    Plus Edna's so skinny,
with her back like a chicken wing,
she hides her wrinkly arms
under long sleeves—tries to, anyway,
but we roll 'em up until Edna feels like
she's falling fast through to nowhere,
but finally she catches on to
how no body who's *worth* somethin'
cares about her arms being wrinkly,
    so she starts coming
      sleeveless in summer

to our back yards that sometimes
only happen in our minds
where we still garden!

Now every so often
we forget
our grandchildren's names,
some of us
never had any children
or no wombs
left either,
   but when we laugh,
      we throw our great arms back
         'til they flop us off balance!

Have you ever
seen cherry tomatoes
like what's growing this year,
so puny with thin skins?
   But the bell peppers!
Why, they hang on by the dozens—
even late in the season, strong winds
can't break them from their stems.
And do you know—inside
the white seeds
  are moist
    and sweet!

Now we've got Edna back
perhaps *you* might like
to stop by some time,
wherever we happen to be,
and see how

those bell peppers
clang like loud hearts

for us sleeveless,
elder ladies!

Old Woman, Earth

Now Earth is slow fire,
travelling toward winter's solstice
in graceful relinquishing
of spring's singing greens
and summer-wet fruit.

Journeying toward a slower,
sparer land
of silk-grey branch and snow-silence,
she is our shape-changer,

Old Woman,
dressed in her vintage clothes,
burnt scarlet, parchment yellows,
and burgundy reds,
she circles the blue-violet sky
around her, a cloud-swirling
shawl of wind!

Autumn fire-bird,
forging a new wingspread
for the longest night,
she is our elegant elder,
close to the edge,
with leaves and twig
dry as old bone,
she kindles the heart
in her fading, golden stove.

About Her Own Body

About her own body,
summer has
no doubts,

she presses you close
with her loose rhythms
and wet loyalties,
while graciously
the sun lets down
its hair,
holding back
nothing.

The light is so strong,
buds break
through the trees'
toughness
to muscle fully
into the world,
and you wonder,
during winter's
hard grip,
is summer a blossom's
most luscious
fantasy,

and do trees
dream?

Even the dirt
is revealing itself,
as roots plunge
deep, deeper
into the yielding dark.

Once more,
faith has bloomed
in Earth's hips
and lifted up
its green and golden praise,

so even you begin
to move again,
like any body
of water
heading towards
its source.

Whatever the losses,
you know,
summer comes
and goes,
but will never
leave you.

I Only Wanted to Be A Boy

for one month,
30 days of longing
and practice
starting when Warren Hasselblad
let me hold his penis
while he peed.

I felt he had a very beautiful
penis for being seven,
his belly was flat
and white like a china plate
below which the delicate stalk emerged
tipped with a fluted and tiny mushroom.
As I held it
between my thumb and forefingers
at a good slant,
we watched
the thin yellow stream,
how bright the porcelain was,
the whole room nodded like the head
of a sunflower.

He showed me how to shake off
the last drops gently,
then he tucked it away.

Standing before the toilet
which was tall as my knees,
later I put up the seat
by myself, leaned in, pointed
my tiny butterfly parts
just like Warren—
and let go.

It wasn't the experience
I had hoped for.

That standing up part, though,
was so satisfying, I studied the situation
and just moved till I was parked
right over the bowl with the clear
water right below me—
and on that try
it was good.

I never sat down
all that golden month,
Warren let me hold his penis
six more times,
then it was August,
time for School, separate bathrooms,
and second Grade,
when they had us choose band instruments,
I wanted to play trumpet
        like Russell Loper
            but they made me
                play flute.

These Mornings of Summer

i.

These summer mornings,
when the linens are languid mushrooms
grown from the forest of our bodies,
carrying our breath, sweat,
our fluids,
in the humid dawn,
these mornings of summer
forget boundaries,
arrive like water
slipping up on us
in and out, in and out,
calling to us
from the inner reaches
of their own muse:
"Wake up, wake up, people,
and create the world!

Unfolding
so bold and sweet,
like the world's first petal,
the fine stem of dawn
spins and roots
from trails
of moonlight,
easing night's intense
body of indigo
to light the leaves
of moist early green,

Morning is so
ready to go,
polishing off our dreams,

driven always
always to be new,
sometimes morning envies our
repetitions, our toil, even our
monotonies and sameness,
prays for us
to gather up each step by step,
another day, another day
press on and bring it home,

To lie down again,
let the day rest,
returning to night
when the spinning stars
excite morning all over again
to wake us
back to the world,
round and round,
pressing on and steady
as bees return
to the unfinished flower
for a deeper drink,
in love
all over again
with the beginning!

ii.
Except when mornings
come on bitter
in the lost and rotten
body of too much
summer
when waking up
is only an end
to sleep's blue-black refuge,
an angel who retreats, leaving

no beauty,
heat has no remorse,

dawn burns the sky
with no mercy,

wasn't there such a morning?

A summer's morning all the fireflies
of last night's Heaven
could not light?

Warm Bathwater

When babies sink into warm
bathwater, they often pee
immediately from the sheer
pleasure of it all, and if
they are little boys
sometimes the jet
of warm urine shoots
straight to their foreheads
  direct and personal as a
    Western Union Telegram.

So says my friend Dave
as we share our lives over tea,
how his boy baby is startled
wide-eyed each time
  the unexpected current
  of himself hits home.

With no son of my own,
my tea cup in midair
I sit breathless
for the facts.
        Dave slips out
these moments easy
as sliding off a log,
just one of his many bath-tub
days and nights,
while I am swept away
  into the immense lap
  of this wild detail.

It comes home to me
more exciting than the stories of Gods,
big as Moses coming down
off the mountain,
   fresh as Aphrodite
    sailing in from the sea.

As suddenly,
and deep I know how
I will love you—
in the water-course way
of baby boys—
turn on the faucets,
let your face unfold,
   your body unfurl,
in miniature gestures
that can't be guessed,
   surprise me—
I want you there
in the odd moment
   beyond trained delight,
the most inside story
when the curve
of warm bathwater
   direct from the heart
   hits home,

   I want you.

My Hair Is A Preacher

I am certain my hair
would make Einstein jealous
if he were alive.
He'd stop all his research
and good deeds
just to shake his unruly head
to match my ragginess,
even beyond death
Einstein would recognize
the Brotherhood
of uncharted locks,
hair more adventurous
than scientific breakthroughs,
as exciting
as the hypotenuse!

Our hair is a stray cat
in wild alleys.
Beyond barretts and maps,
it flaps its night-wings
like owls,
unspeakable hair
that takes you beyond words.
It lights in your eyes
invites you beyond
the asylum
of yourself only.

Yes!
this savage protein
no tamer with a whip

can train,
uncaged,
it falls in my face
like a jungle
you have to sneak through
to get at my eyes.

You say, I am unwieldy,
  You ask: Am I hiding?
    You want, you want,
      you want me to be
        at least, *normal,*
          level-headed.

You want
    You want me to be:
      This is your religion, your prayer.
        Be like you, be like you, be like you.
But my hair is a preacher,
so listen to the gospel,
it's no magic trick.
You don't have to buy a ticket,
  Just wake up, I'm not a room
in a house you own
to redecorate from pictures
in catalogues.
          Just want *me,*
give that tight little
mirror in your heart
a rest,
and my hair will offer you
a ride in its electric thicket
that will carry you to the new world.

Come: dive in.
Strip naked of your hair nets
and your bound feet.
    Face it,
until now
your life has been a burden
like climbing steep mountains
on wings of dragon fly.

But just dare to embrace
my hair
and we will wrap you
in blue fire,
    renew you.

My hair and I
welcome you
with all the little follicles
of our wild heart.

Beyond War or Sin

There is an ancient story that water invented skin so it
could get up and move around in order to experience love.

We are falling
into each other's mouths
love bodies of manna
in the milk and honey night
swollen sweet fruits
of bliss
a blend of soul
beyond shape
or skin, beyond war
or sin
a most divine juice
spilling back through time
even to the Fertile Crescent
and beyond, back to the
purest ancestral
oooooooohhh

We are the world nipple
sucking to know itself
bathed in the first sea's longing
to become Body
be come come we come
come in flows
hot
bright foam
on dark wild water
we yield
to this little death
our ticket to the Beyond
lost,
drowning

in a rest
even beyond sleep

until we drift
back to shore

Is there a holier land
than this love
cradled in our bodies?

Oh, milk and honey night,

Bless us
for we have eaten,

Each of us
a fruit
on the Tree of Life!

Let It Roll Off Your Tongue

A wild and visible
roundness moves before us,
where the belly button rides,
high, testifying above our thighs,
a cave where we emerge
from our ancestors,
a tunnel reaching back
to the curve of birth
and woman,

each of us comes from
and carries
a belly.

BELLY

Let it roll off your tongue!

B which begins.
The breathless E
Generous stretch of LLLLLLL
And, at last, the Y,

How it lifts!

The Belly.

It conjures
warm and rising bread
on puffing radiators
covered with comfy white cloths
that pulsate imperceptibly.

Some bellies rise
more than others.

When they take away
the cloth, these bellies
find themselves

OUTLAWS.

In some dangerous
subtle moment
they crossed the borderline
to alert fear
and wrath
of the Body Police,
the *Belly Politzia*

who frown and point
with harsh voices,

"This is revolting,"

"An excess of flesh,"

"BUSTED FOR EVEN 1 EXTRA INCH!"

They set curfews,
ghettoes,
post grim mandates:

WORK   IT   OFF

"Impure," cry the fascisti:

They sentence these roundnesses
to crawl in shame,
humiliated by mirrors,
fettered beneath beltless huge sweaters,
driven to slant boards
in fluorescent health clubs

or inside
in summer
in desolation at home.

The body police have broken up
the family of the body
exiling this errant part
to public dockets
where they MEASURE,

while a certain pentecostal group
pressures for sanctions
to blazon a red "B"
on bellies of 2 inches or more
for betrayals against society,
crying out:

Brothers and sisters,
this low class round
of too much softness,
this *criminal* calls forth slurs
like "Disgusting," "Ugly,"
"GROSS!"

But at our meeting tonight,
let us truly ask ourselves:
are these insults fierce enough?
Shouldn't we find a fresh new slander
more specialized
for these SINS OF NATURE?

Is not, after all, this uprising
from the middle body
THE ORIGINAL SIN?

Is 'Revolting' degrading enough?

"NO"???

Shall we work on it together—
Find just the right slash
for this embarrassment
of flesh?

My friends,
until next time,
let's sit with it,

Turn that question around.

Why not?

Do we want to live unexamined lives?

Bellies everywhere face for your answer!

They are rising, rising everywhere—
Make no mistake.

Time is of the essence,

For the belly is full,
full of plenty,
full of surprise,

This cornucopia harvested you
from the fields of nothingness.

You will return there soon enough,
and your belly
will vanish
with you.

The Body Radiant

Each of us is a body
of water and fire
body of earth
wind body of breath

Each of us
a natural world

The chemistry of our hair
the maps of our finger tips
are like no other
each chromosome
a galaxy of inner space

When we lie on the earth
spread our arms and legs
in four directions
we are a circle
an etheric body so electric
we radiate energy like a golden sphere!

Yet, magazines created from
the dead bodies
of trees tell us we are not
beautiful enough or whole

They preach our shape is
a fall from grace

urge us   to compare
envy   compare
it is dangerous
to share

They warn: our cup
empties when another fills

BEWARE: these are the power sneaks,
who speak to us with the sound
of our own voices,
whispering inadequacies,
impoverishments,

Whispering:

In another's power, our weakness,
In another's art, our clumsiness,
In another's brilliance, our humiliation
Take care!

The beauty snatchers,
are always in the neighborhood
to invade our dreams

Beware,
Earth needs us
to turn these thieves
out of the temple!

How much time does she have
for us to hide our eyes,
wounded,
in isolation?

Do the voices whisper *"You are shameful"*?

Do they whisper *"Stay hidden"*?

Reach out. You are not alone,

a rare creature,

no other community
of cells like you
on our planet!

Do the voices whisper *"You grow old"*?
Remember the rings of wisdom
accumulated inside us
like a great oak
and celebrate—

the sap is running richer
to carry on!

First body
of our bodies,
Earth needs us
to remember

Each of us is a world,
a history,

Each of us
a doorway

Beware the beauty snatchers,
when the voices whisper:
hairless, wrong-bodied, average, uncherished,
childless, unpublished, unachieved,
failed, incomplete: guilty

LIFT UP YOUR HEAD

We are of her,

Earth

THE BODY RADIANT

Each of us,

A VISION

When Earth looks to us,
she needs to see
our sacred face.

Hard Knocks

Now that I've had three espressos
I'm amped and steamed
and mean, and totally righteous,
I am trying to hold back from putting
into words why
I do not like the word *"TITS,"*
because, knowing myself as I do,
I will no doubt officiously go on record,
turn this into a poem
and imagine someone cares
why I don't like the word,
then if I have time,
I'll move on to *"PRICK"*
and my lack of enthusiasm for it—
the word, I mean.

But you know part of being a poet
is about believing somehow
that one's tiny
private thoughts will catch a ride
to the universal,
and since *"TITS"* is fairly universal
I must go forward and
what I can tell you is this:
only someone who has never cupped
their hand around a woman's breast
and truly felt its round and sweet-tipped vowels,
its swaying waterfall rain-forest flesh
so full of resource, lifting up, in flight,
and precious as the rare eburu jungle bird,
only someone who has never
sensed these things
will get off on *"TITS."*

From the lilt of *"BREAST"* to the
cold edge of *"TIT"*—is this not
the clear-cut deforestation
of a name?
Hard T's
with a little "ih"—

TIT: short, quick, over!
Do people who truly like the word
squeeze what they call
love-making into one hard knock
on the language of the body?

As for *PRICK*
that stabbing "ick"
with a little PR at the start—
I'll leave you to imagine my opinion,
except to say the word has nothing to do
with that elegant column
of enclosed sea and blood
that rises from a man's body
clothed in smoothest flesh
ready to burst with foam
the color of moons.

Larger Than A Good Story

Scheherazade is out for her walk
right through town
with her eyes open.
She has a big name,
a long history of being tricky,
her body is larger than a good story.

Scheherazade passes very near
the huge clear windows
of a fruit market
on the corner,
the towering glass
throbs toward her
on the sidewalk
listing like a glacier
pressing out its course
toward the ample
   Scheherazade
who is so frequently measured,
so often appraised
she sometimes bears
her body
like a stone,
reflected suddenly
in the fruit shop window.

Her complete
body
passes before her
in the market's
vast glass eye

veering toward exposure
Full View
in all her substantial truth.

Riveted,
she stares into the glass
at her image,
as it begins to fuse,
to merge
with the abundant fruits
lined up appealingly inside
against the market's window,
her thighs
indistinguishable
from pomegranate,
her heart ruby flush
as the vivid flesh inside,
her mind plum
and full of juice,

All this fruit
once hanging from the branch
arrived now
to be gathered,
she is a handful
of the finest
on the tree,
unspoiled,
revealed.

So anyone
in their right mind,
might say:

"Scheherazade, you are
a blessed sight,
a true vision
of loveliness."

Instead of eyes
        trained on her
with their trigger
        cocked,
eyes that only follow orders,
hard wired to track
the waxed, perfected, sample body
air-brushed and one day soon
fashioned from all
man-made materials
with no earth left in her.

  But Scheherazade
keeps on walking,
just now she has turned the corner,
her body light all around her
after such a stroke of immanence:
that fruitful moment
when you harvest yourself
with a metaphor that
reaches in deep
and saves you,
fires you up
even while the cold eye
of scrutiny
or the cruelest glass
tries to break you down

to their image
and don't kid yourself,
Scheherazade knows
the world is not safe
  for the real body,
    the body variable,
      her extravagant body,

She knows
    how this world gets mean enough
      to kill off a poem's faith
        and seriously fool with
          your latest revelations.

She will tell you
she knows
how hard it is
to rise up
or even stay awake
in *this* field of poppies.

Scheherazade,
  the abundant,
she has a big name,
a body more prime
than a bushelfull of myths,
she is a footsoldier
out to stand for every precious shape
on the vine.

Scheherazade,
  the fierce,
even when she falters

she remains proud,
therefore mysteriously armed,
as if life depends on it,
she is a vigilante
with her eyes open,

Take her personally,
   her war is Holy,
the whole body
is her Grail.

*The original Scheherazade, in the <u>Arabian Nights,</u>
was one of the wives of the Sultan of India. She
was a warrior who fought the violence against her
with her imagination. She learned that the Sultan
liked to kill each of his wives on their wedding
night, so that evening at bed-time, she told him a
story but withheld the ending until the next
morning. He was so taken with her story-telling
that he spared her life.*

Still Fastened To The Branch

"The present moment
is a powerful Goddess."
Goethe

No one can fool eternity.
True, we may endure,
tough as the tree of winter
leans into the wind,
its torn leaves still fastened
to the branch.
But the water runs
from the head of the creek
toward larger bodies of itself,
as I have flowed
from beyond Time
into this body of forms
and live here
in my flesh,
bone and nerve,
with all of you,
the sky calling out from above,
the earth meeting us
from below,
here we are
in between, as our life
comes through them
and returns.

Their bodies are
in our hands, also,
their lives

at our mercy for
these few moments.
We have just this moment
 to give something back—
 a poem that doesn't brood
 on death, a child who
 feels she is a leaping
flash of endless life,
 who grows up
 to hold out a hand,
 to plant
 a lasting kiss
on the shores of the
 burdened sea,
 the poisoned trees.

Not much time.

With all of you,
I am flowing toward
a larger body
which any time may claim me,
longing to remain,
yet always moving toward
a Vast Change in Lifestyle,
becoming shapeless as
life beyond the body might be,
formless, as an ancient house dress,
with the tree of winter patterned
on its frowsy pockets,
heading
out of time.

I know— soon I'll have
to pack—
just give me
a few more minutes
to learn
how to use
my life.

One last moment,
    to tend the world
        that has held me
        so steadily

            before I slip
            its grasp.

A Soft Place To Fall

A Stream Of Stars

The dragonfly twilight floats in
on transparent wings, so lightly,
over blue hydrangea, trellised vines,
the unfolding iris, and you,
all my loves,
I sit among you,
still, safe,
trees whispering in my ear,
bees plump as the luminous sun
behind me, dipping into the horizon,
even more joyful than I,
my shadow, long, slender,
reaches to the ancestral stone wall,
leaning on itself,
covered over with vines
greener than money or time.
Surrounded by all my loves,
why ever leave this refuge--
honeysuckle life,
pale evening of blossoms,
the gracious breeze,
  everything sways,
    even stones drift,
and when the sun has fallen
into all the honey,

the shadows have returned to night,
I rise above you,
a summer sky
full of Venus,
moon,

and a stream of stars.

A Sense Of Place

Somewhere between time,
the fog slips
out of night into dawn,
like a woman sheltering
her body with robes:
all fruits, mysteries,
shrouded,
inviting imagination
until a bright, rude hand,
the sun,
pulls away
her scarves
sudden,
exposing the unprepared
morning.

I have secrets.

They move just on the
other side
of this world,
which you love,
by never uncovering
what you may never
understand,
you know
too much light
makes me lonely,

so I drift,
misty, folded,
and even sometimes
you fasten the buttons
of my loosening robe.

Full Prayer, July Moon

Full body, deep moon—
luscious Sister floating low,
your palms heavy
with lotus petals and jasmine
come down,
come down,
into us
through the choir of trees
swinging their evening hymn
to the cobalt sky.
Soothe us with cool reflections
from the curved mysteries
of your dark bloom,
flower of night's most divine longing
whose gilded stem
reaches out over the waters,
enter us
from the other side of heat.

Come, ease the edge,
drench our nakedness
with your silky gown
before we give into the city's hot hands—
pull on its siren dress of brake-light red,
showy sequins and glass bits
over tight factory hips
spilling pocketfuls of spoiled
cigarettes and newsprint
while you hang around
the relentless street.

Open your full heart,
let your merciful flowers
drift down
so clean,
so cool.

Family

In The Teeth

"It's a dangerous game,
little sister,"
logging on my land
I warn her,
still as loggers go,
could there be any thief
more winning,
more fluffed,
than this small young rabbit,
soft and sweet
as your earliest toys
who turns up at dawn
in my garden,
all velveteen and aiming
to chop
my coveted perennials
to the ground
for her breakfast,

while other mornings
she takes the fragile lettuce
or heads of petunias
just as they break forth
into bloom.

I wonder,
how much do I have to share
with wild things?

Shall I bring out napkins
and coffee
to go with the lush leafage
of a full Spring's energy

this bunny has felled,
then abandoned,
after just a few bites?

I tell her
the pang in my heart
at every flower
she tears,
about all the little starving bunnies
in China and
how wasteful she is
and especially
about when I was a kid
in Sauk City,
how I hated Mr. Feebles,
our neighbor, who picked off
rabbits in his garden
and sometimes in ours
by leaning out his bedroom window
with his shotgun.

Every so often,
I'd part the bee balm
or the sweet peas,
to come upon
a stiff and lovely rabbit
staring up at all the lettuce
in Heaven,
with the leaves of its final bite
still in its cold smile.

But my rabbit
listens to these stories,
close to me, side by side,
eating steadily,
the yard is her vast and personal salad,

and I, some strange talking flower
that moves and has no roots,
who will probably disappear.

She waits me out.
In the midst of the city,
she has no fear.

Last night, the second full moon
in June was coming on,
a fat, luminous fruit,
making our mouths water
for more and more of life.

Sitting silently on the porch,
I looked out at a movement
in the dark
and stared
into the ringed face
of a hungry racoon
big as the one who last summer
tore up our neighbor's tomcat,
right near our garden,
we never even
found his tail.

It gave me pause,
how we all eat
and die, wondering who
with that intent look
is steadfastly coming after me,
how eating is vicious
and also like prayer,
because we need its strength.

This little ravager,
Ms. Thumper,
who, warm flesh and heart,
relaxes her watch in my garden,
and forgets the enemy,
maybe what we share,
despite our vigilance,
is a moment
of faith:

we will wake up
tomorrow
to more green leaves
and dew,
right in the teeth
of this wild world.

Low Life and Blood Relatives

Unseemly wet
  knob of flesh,
  child's snot ball,
    what part of Earth,
    what Mother
      loves your facelessness?

Mouth-sucking
  where you sit
  or sleep,
    on seedlings, first buds,
    a vengeance of ugliness
    oozing in my garden!

Unsettling protoplasm,
  mud-whale
    small as fingernails,
      slick mystery of grey

State your purpose!

We live together,
  but is
    respect due?
You, sleazy,
low-down acrobat
passionate
to gum holes
in my delicate-veined
lettuce, crisp
harmonious halves of leaf

with unbroken peripheries
of wet-webbed points
  complete, perfect,
    except for you!

My crude
  neighbor,
    my low-life
    third eye,

Earth's balance,
  wholeness, too,
    is grounded
    in our strange
    difference.

Remind me,
  with your alien body
  of startling goo:
    We are mud relatives.

      We're family,
        me and you.

Ode To Mud

The silent ground has meditated
all these months with the stillness
of monks, until now, lowly singer
of spring, you swing us slowly
toward lilacs and loosenings,
Oh, rhapsody of mud!

Revelation of worms,
ancestral household of bulbs
who brew up their fresh repertoire
in your darkness,
Most grand sogginess,
you release our ground-shifting
moment of truth,
as we place one careful pastel foot
with grace, to stay clean,
only to step in a plotch
of softening-earth
our winter eyes have missed,
and we come,
fumbling,
into your wet wisdoms.

High musician of murk,
teach us to move deftly
as a jazz player's fingers
on a fretless bass
through this improvisation
of raptures,
while winter's kittens
in the new outdoors
explore moist-mysterious
paw-disturbing grass,
before learning to slip with legato stealth

through indigo thickets of April's iris;
the grand divas of mud-country,
pigs,
play your twelve-tone textures
on their bristly backs;
sodden-swaying cows
sink knee-deep
in the fluent fields where sap-tappers
slog toward new-running maples
on higher ground,
each wet step emerges
heavy, heavier, until they arrive,
a crowd of Wisconsin big-foots,
to gather the pure-flowing crystal
that tastes like bliss!

Oh, divine lowliness,
reservoir of rain in the park
where a child dressed in violet boots
and a pale blue sky tries out
her first mud-legs,

before the torch-song sun
woos new-sown seeds,
warming you to summer-dust,
we surrender to your earth-yielding
comings anew!

We are winter stones
released from the tight ground
who fly around the flood-swollen creek
in high winds
under thunderclouds,
then fall back
to a full-bodied waltz
in your damp embrace.

Such Clean Nights

The truly
realized
cat
waits
until you are about
to enter
your first dream
before initiating
its bath,
communion
of tongue and fur,
just as you are drifting
out to sea
with Wynken, Blyncken,
and Nod,
cozy and full of
lullabies,
the fully
revealed
cat
intensifies rhythms,
full-throated purr,
rocking your bed
in its moist
and thorough ceremony,
with vigorous little bites
to punctuate the electricity
of such clean nights,
    this loyal
ritual as constant
as the tides

or faith
must take place
on our nearly calm
and drowsy
bodies
which emanate a peace
so
intoxicating,
cat fur
quickens,
the rough tongue
awakens
from its ordinary
day, and now
in the stillness
we have prepared,
the cat,
in its gratitude,
begins.

Somewhere deep in us we know,
we have given
over the night,
so what can we do
but fall back onto
our pillow,
look out the window
at the shadows of trees
shaking in the wind,
relinquish all resistance,
and go
for the big
picture:

the cat is fundamental,
unmatched in integrity,
never falling away from
its needs,
everyday, the model
of essence.

No more than Michelangelo
could stay his brush from
the Sistine's ceiling,
or the spider
still its silk,
the cat
cannot
turn back,
as surely as the North Star
anchors the sky,
our luscious and sleepy body
steers the cat
home.

Glycerine And Rose Water

The locusts rub up a thunderous din in their late
summer mating while I lie waiting for sleep in the same
bedroom my Mother and before her my Grandfather
and Grandmother returned to after each day, where
they, too, drifted off to this same orchestra rhythmically
circling us together in time.

This was a home. The closet still holds the mothy odor
of Grandpa's suits; when I open the walnut dresser,
glycerine and rose are there, ghosts of my
grandmother's hands, gloves, underclothes. She was
soft, plump with sweeping breasts, so much the round
essence of grandmotherness that anyone thin called
Grandma caught me back and didn't seem right. Could
a grandmother be bony? Even the pale milky brown ace
bandages on her knees added to her soft surfaces.
Grandma Pearl made her gentle, round body a gift.

Grandpa was slim, and well pressed, his pants
impeccably creased down the front with cuffs which he
hitched carefully. I knew not to climb on his lap.
Sometimes he let me sit in the space between his legs
but this was hard on him. People would say until the day
he died, "That Louie Schultz was a fine, dapper
gentleman." I knew his love would turn up in different
ways. So I went to Grandma whose wide lap was
usually open. Louie was all bones and fine-combed hair.
Sunday mornings when he paced, waiting to be picked
up for Mass, he'd often touch the clean pink part
separating his white hair to make sure he was spruced
up just right for God. Always he worried he'd be late,
and always he ended up worshipping exactly on time.

My Grandmother stayed home— she was not a
churchgoer—making coconut pie so sweet it made
Sunday sprout wings. After Grandpa prayed to save his
soul, back he came to have his special drink before
Sunday supper— "I think I'll just have one of them
thangs," he'd say: ice he'd break up in an old hand
crusher, rusty and slow; then one shot dry Vermouth,
one shot whiskey, pinch of bitters, and when I was
visiting two red cherries he'd soak for me. We'd sit in
the tiny sunroom's rockers, he'd sip, rattling the ice and
I'd rock sometimes an eternity until he'd lean over with
his toothpick heavy with those brilliant cherries bitter
from liquor, yet sweet, too.

At supper, after briefly sitting with us, Grandma would
rise and lurk, waiting to sweep away our plates, eager to
display the pie—a dark gold crust just fringing pale
quivering yellow custard which when presented to the
mouth contained small sweet bursts of coconut. Later
after dishes, which I'd wash over again sometimes, old
as he was, Grandad would miss a few specks and
remnants, Louie and Pearl would go off to the bedroom
for a rest, in the Sunday stillness of the afternoon.

I'd sit outside or lie in the grass on a blanket keeping the
ants company, while the sky opened over me, one vast
blue bloom where small white moths of cloud briefly lit.
The bees would burrow in the moss rose, the trees lazily
swing their leaves. And sometime later, while I slept, my
grandmother would get up, go to the bureau, splash
glycerine and rose water on her face, neck and hands.
As she came near to rouse me, calling me "Precious," I
woke up amazed the garden roses were dreaming only of
me.

Old Louie Schultz

At 99,
Old Louie Schultz
feels the slight breeze
blow right through him
even on
hot afternoons,
bones of
his cheeks
shine through
from the other side.

Some days he drifts like
an old spider's web come
unhinged from its corner
out in the shed:

>"*Can't tell if
>I'm on land or sea,*"

> he hoists his cane
> like a sail.

Some days he plans.

Next Spring,
he wants to try
yellow tomatoes
and *"Startling Vertigo,"*
Burpee's latest rose
and he'll place his bet
on the race horse,

"Man of War,"

"Heaven's not ready
for me yet!"

Come planting time
Louie bends again
to poke in his seeds,
spreading a veil of loose earth,
then lightly waters.
   He sticks his cane
in the damp ground,
pulls himself back up,
an old pod
waiting for the wind.

   Earth shifts,
suddenly,
he fumbles,
keeling
onto his side,
   looks up,
   the sky becomes
   a whirling pool
   of light.

After sleeping in his own bed
for nearly a century,
the nursing home
seems
like a ghost ship
far, far away
from his
own backyard.

Old Louie Schultz sails
and spins
on a startling sea
of glistening flowers
where horses' hooves
beat the surf
as he drifts
through his senses:
"Dying takes a lot of doing."

One day
at nap-time
he pulls himself up,
wondering why Pearl
hasn't come to bed,
slips over the bedside
onto the cool floor
and floats,
   wide-eyed
like he's just seen
Heaven's first rose.

Such A Stink-Pot

Right after surviving
my oral book report
on the Hindenburg Blimp
in sixth grade,
during my Disaster period
when I loved hearing about things
going up in flames,
people screaming,
with on-the-spot reporters,
"O, my God, O, my God," over
and over,
I was walking back
to my seat,
dropped my report,
bent over,
and the carefully folded
kleenex
in my bra
fell out
right by Terry Collins'
desk, and he dutifully
reported on the spot
before he held up the kleenex
for the entire class
to see,
*"Boy, you really
have a lot of blackheads
in your nose,"*

I wondered
how anybody

ever wanted to marry
such a stink-pot
as a *boy.*

So I asked my Mom
that night if I had to
get married,
and why did she?

She answered: *"How
did your book report go?"*
I looked out the window, then,
at the huge oak tree
I often climbed in for answers
because it had a great view
of the neighborhood,
and the Catholic steeple,
but this was a question
my solitude, I knew
would not settle.
I decided to go next door
to Joe and Mary Tison's house
to see Joe
who'd had polio so long
all he did was lie in a hospital bed
with his bones shining through his skin
and his wife, Mary, always asking,
"Do you need anything, Joe?"
over and over, year after year,
and above his bed, this crucifix
with Jesus on it,
who I knew never got married,
and even his Mother had

by-passed Joseph,
but Mrs. Tison, you could tell
she loved Joe, truly,
every time she brought him
a 7-Up
and sat for hours with him,
watching
Joe McCarthy go
after Communists
on the tiny black and white T.V.—
she'd grab the railings of the bed,
"That man just makes me mad enough
to spit,"
and Joe would say,
"Now don't go raising your
blood pressure, Mary,"
real sweet, in a voice that
wasn't getting enough air.

I sat there by the bed-side,
on my own, studying them,
it was so confusing,
Terry Collins, Joe Tison, and Jesus,
and Joe McCarthy,
Mary and Joseph,
and my Mom not having
much to say
about love
except this strange
demolished look
she gave me
as if maybe a passenger jet
was about to fall
from the sky,

like the one that grazed
our chimney last winter
and crashed right down
the block
which I found exciting
but my Mom pegged
as **"a very close call."**

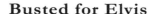

Busted for Elvis

Somewhere in the 50's
I got in big trouble
after sneaking out
to Elvis's early movie,
"KING CREOLE,"
and my mother grabbed me
soon as I got back
with her frightened eyes,
she said I was a liar
and doomed
to lust
while I tried to understand
from her hard grip
all my sins.

What I wanted to tell her
was that after
"KING CREOLE,"
Pat Boone was OVER for me—
BOOM,
like a fatal accident
whereas before I'd been glued
to WOKY AM Radio
waiting everyday for
Pat to croon
"Ain't That A Shame"
in his tied-up saddle shoes voice.

Pat Boone was over.

Elvis had Delta Hips and New Orleans

in his phrases,
he woke me up
when I didn't know
I was sleeping,
I was grateful to be busted
for Elvis and even if
Elvis was dangerous,
I knew he was right for me.

Who she should have been scared of
was Paul Newman as *Ben Quick*
in "THE LONG HOT SUMMER,"
a movie my Mom *took* me to,
when he says
to Joanne Woodward:

"Miss Eula, the world is made up
of meat eaters, and if you want
to make it in this world,
you have to like to eat."

But when Elvis hung out on the Porch
and this Black woman cried out "Crawfish"
and Elvis sang back with his throat
full of early morning and the streets
they made me want to kneel and howl
just for the glory
of being in life.

That's what I would've
told my Mom, back then,
but I was twelve.

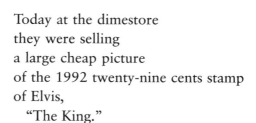

Today at the dimestore
they were selling
a large cheap picture
of the 1992 twenty-nine cents stamp
of Elvis,
   "The King."

Suddenly I wanted to buy it
so bad it surprised me
but then, just as surprising,
I flipped back to when

I was 15 and found out all about
race records and how all
the Black singers got no
white air time,
how the handlers
were looking for a white singer
with a Black sound,
and how
it wasn't exactly fair
Elvis being called "The King,"
because his roots were owed
to Black music.

I got busted for Elvis
all over again
because could I love him
and be fair to the Bluesmen
Jimmy Witherspoon
or Joe Turner or
how about Bessie Smith
who died from a car wreck

because no white hospital
would take her.

So things looked different at 15
about who I had the right to love
and how to listen to my heart
and be just,
when I was going crazy
for the Blues.

I knew today
when I couldn't buy Elvis' picture
right off that I'm still mixed up
about my part in Justice,
how to help pay up all these dues,
like Elvis says to Carolyn Jones
in "King Creole," "I gotta
lot of payin' back to do,

a LOT of payin' back."

It's not so simple and blind
like the 50's
when I could just walk away
from Pat Boone for the King.

So maybe I'll go back for
Elvis's stamp picture, after all,
but put him underneath my photograph
of Ellington's Orchestra playing
"The Mooch."

Then I go back to
my Mom's panic

about how Elvis
was the dangerous outlaw
OTHER, he was "bad" music,
    he'd crossed the borderline,
and I forgive her because
what's returning to me now
are the people who took it way beyond
her fears,
the white guys full of
family values who went
on T.V. to preach that Elvis'
music was, and I *quote:*

"Clearly a way to
bring the white man and his children
down to the level of the Nigger"
and how Elvis got death threats
and they put out the rumor
he shot his mother,
until Ed Sullivan made a point
to say he was a "good, decent young man."
But they only gave him waist-up
shots on T.V. after that,
because when they heard
all that soul and saw how he felt
the rhythm
all they could see
was sex: *"Vulgar, animalistic,*
Nigger Rock,"

even thirty years later
they're making this poem
ugly.

No way
for Elvis to win,
dropped as he was
into hundreds of years of bad history
too few "I'm sorry's"
from the white fathers,
with no reparations.

Elvis mooched,
  he used,

  he was used,

night after night
he could not sleep,
   died young,
keeps
coming back
white spirit gilded with blackness
still restless to touch
this world
full of
a *whole lotta dues*
and too little
   gratitude.

The Plush Body That Poured Me

Once I floated,
  a huge bubble,
in the dark space
  of you, hooked up by

The long slick cord,
  relentless
    to burst out
      and move on.

Later when I lay
  on your sweating body
    we began,

      Without direction,

        New darknesses
          and light.

Now while the doctors
  so somberly
    show me your X-rays,
the smoky shadows
  and thickening white,

I fade back to see you
  in other photographs,
    younger,
      bare-armed, full-bloomed
in cotton white
  and violet dresses

from the 40's,
  loose and smiling
    on wide blankets in parks.

You end here
  on this bed
    white as the oldest seashell,
    almost dust.

The cord hooked
  in your hand
    holds you by a thread,

    When suddenly your eyes
    fly open
      out of your final dream,

    And you say,
    "Blow harder!"
    and I imagine

    You might mean
    the time you
      taught me the power

    Of my breath
    was like the wind,
      blowing the puffs

    Of dandelions
    until the silk
      took to the air,

Or are you asking God
to free you?

And soon your eyes
stay open
looking into forever,

The spirit
rushes out
and what is left
of the plush body
that poured me into
this life

Is one thread
of silk
that will easily
ride the wind.

This Dead Calm

Every cell in my body
has a song.
When you left,
all melodies
fell to their knees,
bereft,
and have remained
silent,
still
no revival.

Where are you?

This quiet without mercy,
    this dead calm.

    Wait, *is that a sound,*
your phantom heart
still beats in me,
not I, not you,
    we were our body,
a whole life,
    and now
    a constellation
that has lost its stars,
huge vault
in the mute night,
my eyes open,
staring, sleepless,
into forever, *ever, ever,*
I am space,

only space between notes
that simply hang above
emptiness,
 trembling unbearably.
How can I never
hear again,
the song of your voice
calling my name?

Womb-Rider to The Death

Suspended near
  my Mother's heart,
    I learned early
      how to swim,
        a womb-rider,
          her rhythms setting
            my first vibrations,
            my electricity,

first, an ovum
  pooling chromosomes,
    zygote subdividing to tadpole,
      the shape of an ear
        I sank into the soft tissue
          of her swelling pouch,
            bobbing about,
              a primal question mark
until I slipped out
    on a chilly night
    with thighs
  the size of thumbs
  six weeks too early
    in Tennessee
      where you, Mother, were
        "the only grey-haired one
        in maternity."

  "I was afraid when I carried you,"
    you confided later,
      "the last weeks in bed,
        hanging on.

At night a nice hillbilly girl
with dirty red braids
would come, brush
my hair and say,
'Why, Miz Loveridge,
you sure is old for babies!' "

And when you told this story,
you'd always say, *"Your father was . . ."*
and then you'd pause, *"Well,*
away in California on some
hair-brained scheme,
never did know what
it was, except he came
back with his pockets empty.
So sometimes I would stoke the fire
myself. Even Tennessee has
a cold November."

So how did your heart beat,
 Mother, as I changed shapes
 inside you.
                What vibration
        sounded
                your loneliness?

You felt so watery,
 Earth seemed to drift.
 I floated
            in your longing.

Did you ever know balance,
 while I sought land

for years,
registering your heart's
drowning,

you clung to me,
tiny jetsam
in dark waters
lit by the moon.

You had an enduring dream
you would tell me
some mornings at breakfast:
"There's a train I run for,
keep missing, again, and again.
I run to get my baggage,
when I come back—
train's gone."

We sat at the table,
mystified together.
Your larger life lived ahead
of us like a lustrous
sailing ship moving toward
brilliant sun, so dying

you said: *"I've never*
felt so free,"

and you, who rarely spoke
of God, thanked God
"For everything."

At the end,
you let go

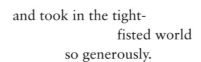

and took in the tight-
                    fisted world
        so generously.

You reached out to me,
    wide-armed,
        and I swam back to you.

I still sense your early pulse
    when I lived in
        your warm,
            frightened waters.

But as you left,
    your heart opened
        with final gifts—

        I travel in the echo.

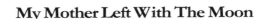

My Mother Left With The Moon

my mother's death, at the time
of a total lunar eclipse, 1981

How can the night and day
ever be the same
when the world falls and falls,
dead weight with no spin,
I dream, Mother,
the universe is mourning you
so hard,
even the stars have lost
their place,
and gone gambling.

The dragon sky has eaten
the whole moon,
orphan tides wander along the shores
where phosphorous flung onto sand
glows as though
a transient galaxy of tinkerbells
lights up a summer midway:

Step right up, ladies and gentlemen,
under the big top, to see Infinity,
our prize gambler, steal the show!
Watch him roll those dice!
Sure he looks tuckered,
he's won all the horizons
but lost the twilight in just one night.

Friends, step right over here
into Space—regard our ferris wheel!
See where Time rides the highest cars,
feet dangling in the dark,
no safety bar in this free-fall night?

O, we're sorry to say the moonlight
is nowhere to be found,
we've lost her,
she's dead, run out of town
by the free-wheeling drifter,
Earth, who is, some say, nearby
on a wild ride in the hungry sky.

Friends, have no fear, step right
over where the stars are running
a brisk business, backed up, we admit,
by an edgy eternity who, ladies and gents,
we may have to fire soon,
since
we lost
the moon.

True, the moon is gone,
still, the Milky Way plays on,
like always,
hawking the classiest program
in its diamond-white and sequin
evening suit. Like always
the Milky Way plays on, and on.

It's the original big-time
big-top show.
But the moon,
my friends,
is gone.

Going Whole

I love Forehead lifts.
  They smooth the face out.
  More importantly,
  they put the brows in the right place."
    Dr. Toby Mayer, plastic surgeon, Beverly Hills

I saw an old, old Hopi woman's nose—
an eagle on the promontory
of her face,
and remembered
my Great Grandma Sherman's
skin, earth without rain,
full of twilight.

Now I am journeying on,
ripening,
I am the geography
of all my ancestry,
I'm bound for the elements!
Blue shadows enter
the slopes
of my cheeks.
I am sky,
  my eyes
    moving toward cloud.

What will I become?

Dry sand over seeds of desert corn?
A moist furrow or turbulence underground?
You see, there is a giving-back,
a shift.

Also a gathering.
I am fertile in these changes,
fertile like stone,
like a canyon
whose steep walls and ridges
house spirits of "the old ones"
who once lived nearby
and passed on.

I am my blood-line,
my Grandpa, Louis Schultz,
Tom Loveridge, and Louise,
Grandma Pearl, and Great Grandmother
Sherman, the oldest woman
I ever knew,
curve of light and shadow
in her high-backed rocker,

community of lives,
    a wheel losing its power.

    All my old ones are gone.

Still I am their place of return,
their homestead.
My Mother's arms that weathered me,
mapped with the markings
of decades
and full of familiar places to visit
are now my own.
    If my nose is fixed,
or tip of chin swept up past my mouth,

and tucked,
will I lose some family, too,
some groove or hue?

Will my father's light tenor
on "Danny Boy,"
still echo along some horizon
of my ears,
     Aunt Rusty's southern-lady
voice when she'd say:
"Honey, you've just got to rub up
when you put on make-up,
to keep your cheeks
young"

will they be pruned
with my lips?

Never! I tell you,
I am going whole,
standard-bearer of their full age,
and mine,
remembering Great Grandma Sherman
so ancient
she was just a shimmer
before the windows in our family room,
a curtain our future shone through,
whose once full-blown body
was the soil for this woman,
     as you see me: Louisa.

My Mother's Lover's 95th Birthday

Old Edwin Canfield has a great big
wrought iron
fish hook right over
his front door, ready
to snag a good fish,
says they need 'em
that big down here
in the Ozarks
but much as he knows about
fishing
way long ago in 1922
he couldn't catch my Mom,
hard as he tried.

Edwin was short and spare,
plain as a bone button
when he was 19
and normal as milk,
Louise was after bigger
fancier game,
not a boy who would live
and die in a Missouri Valley,
no country boy
for her but a fast-talker
in a brim hat from St. Louis
charmed her silly
so my Mother
slipped Edwin's hopes
for a pretty man
who, as it turned out,
never let truth get in the way

of a good story,
he swept her right
into a hard life,
but Edwin had a good country memory
that never filled up
with the city's noise,
he could still remember Louise's voice
much later, long after their families
had grown,
she returned home, alone,
to the Valley, she was plump,
hair thin as milkweed,
but Edwin heard the same lilt
in her voice that 75 years
had not changed,
he showed up
at her screen door again,
wooed her
like only an old man could,
fast, no time wasted,
with true love,
seemed like it wasn't
but a few months,
after too few heavenly nights on the couch
playing scrabble,
conversations full of delight
and Edwin's persimmon wine,
she slipped his grasp again,
took sick and died. Death had no
respect for the love
left in them.

Today, when I phoned
Edwin on his 95th birthday,
he choked up:
"I dreamt about your Mother
just last week,"
I asked could he tell me
but he said it was
"too personal"
and I wonder how
could my Mom
pass up a man
who still dreams
about her down
through the years,
     and years,
beyond her whole life,
or any poem,
he clasps the mystery of her so close
this time she didn't
get away.

Divining

It was cloudy bright and
shadowless that day.
The geese gaggled overhead,
seeking water in their divining way,
the marsh grass moved with the winds,
soft grasses so rust and purple grey
while the milkweed burst with silk.
Oh, how my lover covered me deep
near the marsh waters,
and the dead tree
seared by fire stood close by.
The poles of earth and sky
held us in a balance so vast,
we wept
and lay, the silk filaments of the
milky weed
falling weightless.
Pressed against the whirling
Earth we rocked
in the rust and purple grey
seeding the ground, while the geese
flew overhead
in their divining way
and my lover covered me deep
near the marsh waters.
Oh, ours was a milky love
that could not tire,
close by, my dear, rose the dead tree
seared by fire.

Dearly Beloved

Talk to me.

Even our plants
are not letting on
when they need water.

The light slanting through
our blinds
is brittle as parchment
that's survived fire.

All the loose threads
of the afghan on this old couch
where we sit and sit
are full of secrets.

Why do you listen
to yourself
like an echo?

Are you straining to hear
what you might dare to say?

Come, tell me
the unspeakable.

Or how will we move
through the next gateway?

Already our eyes carry
the empty water vessels
of wanderers in deserts.

Time is an old bone
drying in the sun.

Come. Reach inside
and love me,
us,
from the relentless
truth.

I will meet you there.

Do You Know

I have folded my arms
around a maple tree
running heavy with sap
touched my lips
to her rough bark
and sipped clear light
from her dark body.

I have lain down
in the desert night
when the sky embraced
so many stars I cried in their arms
from ecstasy.

When you left,
I banished these joys,
Oh, I gave them all away.

I have lost babies,
buried loved ones,
searched for my Father's grave
unmarked, among
the granite tombs
of strangers.

When you left me,
these sufferings became
a distant mist,
they were easy weather.

Do you know,

there was no sap
to taste,
no tree in spring
or desert sky,

no trace of me
but passion's rag.

A Soft Place To Fall

*"Adama" (Adam) from the Hebrew "earth" or
"soil"; "Hava" (Eve) from the Hebrew "living"*

Please,
lay down a love
that is some fine dirt,
rich with earthworms
so it breathes like a good pair
of lungs, full of song,
where the prayers
of all seeds
are answered,
  a soft place
   to fall,
    down and down,
until I empty myself
in an untiring rain,
   under,
     around me,
       the good soil,
where I can truly
lie down,
small, ephemeral,
facing the blank sky,
   stay with me,
     loosen my garment
     of spent blossoms
       and such loneliness.

Let me sink onto
your steady earth,

the little stones
around us
are pieces of stars
or ancestors who already
know this melancholy
is only a season,
they won't let me sleep
too deeply.

I am so tired.

Keep up your music,
song of the dirt,
keep singing,
lift up
your instrument
until the sprouts
raise their arms
through your surfaces
until I almost hear again
the breezy eighth notes
of praise.

My love,
this breathing earth
that holds fast
to a rhythm
even while it spins,
hold me a little longer,
    longer,
then thrust me up
to carry on
above ground
once more.

Just A Plain Fool

Some days I'm just
a plain fool,
no cup
seems full enough,
no fire

Richard Gallas

in my
body
burns hard enough.

   I yearn.
     I cry out:
       "I am not enough,"

call for more belonging,
endless and
pure.

I want the trees
to swing in the wind
just for me,
  the crickets to rub
their legs together
in my praise,
  to be the only image
in the loon's red eye.

I need the edge,
to become the prey of a hawk
who cares just for me
from two miles up
before its swoop
to Earth
now that I'm in its sights.

Then you return
through the doorway
of my longing,
undomesticated,
free, steady as geese
flying home

after hard weather,
and I know
you are the most
reliable wildlife
I need.

Yum

Mmmmm,
Nas...tur...tium,
full of vowels and
ur and um,
is full of delicious sound
and bears a flower
you can eat.
Its life begins
inside a sturdy
seed cover
fluted and wise
as a tiny brain
with great timing,
deep inside,
where for awhile
it is always night,
so the imminent nasturtium

louisa

has fantasies,
dreaming
how the seed cover
will release
at the choice moment
to thrust its bloom
into the world
like the flipper
in pinball
sends balls rolling
so all the bells ring,
all the gates open!

Just like this:

let me germinate
in the underground
of your hips
until the earth moves
and I burst into light
perfect,
and right on time.

Some Thunder In My Comfort

So, old love,
old haunt,
you want to be some thunder
in my comfort.
Stay away from me;
I want you.

You are the debris of ripe memories,
who leaves me with a freight
of longing, abandoned, grown-over,
where every season the weeds
are still beautiful.

Old cans, tires are strewn around,
signs say "Keep Out"—
still I'm back,
retrieving the rhythm
when our train swung
through our private country-side,
together travelling untouched places,
the lost back yards of towns.

You're like the old frame houses
my family passed through
on the road
where I was raised,
so many, they seemed
to be over-night sleeper cars
on *The Hiawatha,*
always moving, except for the gardens
where for a Spring
the sweet peas bloomed,
and some Falls we even harvested
the yellow squash.

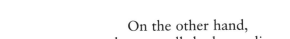

On the other hand,
slugs got all the broccoli,
storms brought down the corn.

The place was heavenly,
but just—didn't work out.
We moved on.

Now I am here, at last,
planted, making a home.
Don't let me hear that lost train swinging
through my back yard with its shadow-sound:
"If only . . .if only . . . if only."

Old haunt, don't visit me.
I love you.

The Kindly Apocalypse

The Kindly Apocalypse

If our world's got to end,
let it be a kindly apocalypse,
one where we can carry good memories
in pastel photo albums,
as we stream into eternity!

Couldn't THE END
be full of promise?
A smash hit
like that dazzling moment
when the dinosaurs,
those Immense Chosen Ones,
looked up to see
the final meteor
rushing toward them
like the great ball of Karma,
forcing all life suddenly
to pierce their vision
in revelations of dinosaur satori!

AHA! They grasp so completely
in the pressure of that speeding moment
how sweet life is,
how full of grace
to tear fresh leaves
from trees fed by sunlight.

If our world is to end,
let it be, simply, a dashing apocalypse,
a fireball of neon
that tattoos one final "Happy New Year"
on the strip mall of flesh
that was our Earth.

Yes!
Bring on
the Supreme Moment of Nature
when Buddha and even God
go gliding into fresh galaxies
giggling through all the stop signs
with a dreadful joy.

When all cross streets
of nihilism and despair
flow suddenly with bread,
wine and 10,000 fishies
JUST BEFORE THE LIGHTS GO OUT!

Couldn't it be like *"On the Waterfront"*
when Brando says to his brother
who set him up,

"Why'd ya make me throw
the fight, Charlie,
I coulda took him.
I coulda been somethin'
I coulda had class,

But face it, Charlie,
I'm a bum
on a one-way trip
to Palookahville."

Couldn't we go that way,
a class-act movie finish apocalypse
where the survivors say
cool things from the Bronx
about *"How life ain't fair,*
Charlie?"

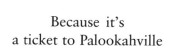

Because it's
a ticket to Palookahville
for us, Chum,

What we got now is
a slow twisting
in the rotten air,

But, Charlie,
we coulda been *'somethin'!*

Old Prophet

Full of warning,
Coyote walks the rocks,
old wary eyes. Beneath his skull,
ancient membranes
celebrate water, then fur,
remembering his long, slow crawl
out of the sea-womb into air,
naked rodent acquiring
spine and claw.

His eye is on us,
the hard ride of evolution
in his dark pupils,
Coyote walks
sharp rock, beneath his skull
fish memories quiver: humid
goggling eyes, transparent gills,
silver-bright body and mouth-sucking;
remembers one cell with a tail,
tremulous cloud in the sea-womb.

Coyote thrusts his neck
into the sky,
cloud-swell breaking,
Coyote's high laugh
warns clouds, the sky-runners,
warns lightning, the sky's claw
and thunder voice,
warns fiery earth-throats
in the red-hot mountain:

"It is time for a ceremony!"

Lightning sets the rhythm

for his ritual dance
at earth's rim,
sounds from his throat
break open stone,

Coyote dances,
lean haunches,
he dances
until the rocks become a supple
flaming sea,
he dances
until darkness swells
to a wild star-stream
until the thunder night
is a sweeping-down flood
that rolls over the burning sea
and puts it out!

This is his warning
to the horizon,
to our next step
out of hot water:

You are not alone,
You better stay on my side,
Coyote sings to us.

Coyote cools,
fire-eyes,
shape-changer, dancer
old prophet,
Coyote is cool
old water-carrier to the life-hoop
maybe.

Why, Just Now

"That we are ignorant of 90% of our own
galaxy and probably of the universe
as a whole is a profoundly unsettling thought."

Space research scientist, Smithsonian Magazine
discussing allocated funds to measure vast
distances in space.

Why, just now,
are you measuring
the Milky Way?

Why spend fortunes
on vortexes separated
from you by light years
when Earth is crying
for your presence?

Why seek the Milky's depths,
just now, during
Apartheid Armageddon
AIDS emergency Ozone Apocalypse?

Will the Holy Grail
of your calibrations
bring grace to one
pregnant poisoned otter
dying in the toxic sea?

Can you see the blood
of the people through

the lens of your telescopes
or our constellations
of fallen children
and vanquished species?

Down here, on the streets,
our kids do their own research,
like how to properly coat bullets
with teflon to penetrate
bullet-proof vests,

They say the "Future"
is just a six-letter word
for "SUCKER,"

While you GREAT ABSENT FATHERS
are slamming back
shots of the Universe
at the New Vistas Bar.

Do you worry
that our galaxy
somehow lacks the goods—
is not big enough
to satisfy?

When we have documented evidence
that our very own Milky Way
can thoroughly fulfill
any other galaxy attracted to it.

As the most recent
research proves

through a survey
of 19 large universes.

Each of them, when asked,

"Was it good with the Milky Way?"

responded: **"It Was The Best Ever!"**

The Milky Way is carrying on!

Cosmic calibrators,
  come home.

Do not measure space
when our own inner life
lies before us
more alien, unsettling,
undiscovered
than the fount of the Big Dipper.

Just now, let endlessness
be endless.

Let pods of stars
leap across your vision
and hot young nebulae
flare untamed.

O, grand measurers,
just now,
let space be unfathomable.
Fold up your tools.

Return to us
where the shuddering
continents,
where the wasting bodies
and siren streets
will welcome you
with a hungry jubilation
no instrument of yours
can grasp.

Space seekers,
  come home.

What Is The Sound

If a virgin tree
  is felled
    in the forest
      does it make a sound
        the logger can hear?

Is there one moment
  of its fall
    through the air
      that registers
        in the delicate hairs
          of his rough ear?

Does the plunder of ancient,
    ancestral timber
    tumbling down
      in a firmament of loss
        reach the glittering
          star of his eye
            as he glories over the final roll
              of the tree's huge body
                after the thunderous kill?

What is the sound
  that will tell him
    the sap draining from
      the raw stump
        of this life
          he has subdued
            is his own blood?

And then there is the sound,
the soft, muddled sound,
of young children's bodies
as they fall
in the rainforest streets,
dead as clear-cut saplings.

The murdered trees
the young dead,
what if they joined
together,
in the same moment
rose up alive again
together,
an apocalypse
that runs backward
until trees overtake
all cement
of the malls,

come piercing through
the gun shops,
the corporations,
isolated mansions
of aloof elite, shattering
security gates and
their antique eggshell china!

Imagine
this milennium,
the trees take back their land
while the young
rise up from where they have fallen,

the bullets travel back
to the guns,
guns fly
to the gun-runners,
the gun-runners become
children again
playing hide and seek
before bed,
drugs return to
fields of poppy
to shine in the dew,

until the trees stand tall
sheltering the young,
simply
being alive,
together,

they are all back
with us,
they make a joyful sound,
full of gratitude
that since none of us
has found an answer,
too many of us
have turned our backs,
too few are sharing the work
and the pain,
therefore,
the trees,
in their power,
the trees,
in their mercy

take life back
into their own hands,
save themselves
and raise the children
back from the dead.

Perhaps this is what
the last remaining tree
on the block
or hillside
imagines,

perhaps this is what
trees dream.

Zahor

*There are things in this world
  that break the heart,
    There are things in this world
    that exalt the soul.*
      Jewish Prayer Book

To Anne Frank, 1929-1945

Far from the moon's sight,
you were closeted in Amsterdam,
an adolescent wondering about her period
while the Nazis named you "bad blood,"
Anna, anybody's neighbor girl;
I was a war baby still dark
in the womb, dreaming of liberation,
my father built war guns
too late for you,
and somewhere Eastern mystics
crooned: "Everything is one
and the play of God's love,"

while winged helmets, and souls
in luger shapes
flew through night
to tell your final
bed-time story.

Today, you would be 56 years old.

Now on your birthday,
I remember,

think on love,
life's purpose, or God.

How to go on
when your story carries me
like a womb,
and everyday I am
a war baby.

To go on,
  to bear hope,
    to go on,
I must step back
from the terrible knowledge
of your interrupted life,

yet still remember.

May this poem witness
all the cutting off
of lives
happening
at this moment.

May this poem join
all other poems that
burn history
into our presence,
like smoke
from death camps
stays in the sky
in photographs.

War anywhere
is war here,
and we are all
war babies.

"ZAHOR."
    "Remember."

August, 1985, Forty years after

Life Ain't All Bad

Absolutely true story—
Our neighbor, Ponch, has got his old cat out
on its leash on the picnic table,
nose up in the air, catching the breeze.
This kitty is just fur over some old bones,
with a strange meow that howls,
and if another cat prowls around,
a little hiss left in him.
Do you believe the old cat made it
through the winter—
This Ponch
is one good guy, let me tell you,
as for example, a bunch of years ago,
this same cat, they call him Wojo,
got out of his collar, came underneath the fence,
and was tearing up our cat, Lucky,
Ponch threw himself over the fence
between our yards—
Mind you,
that thing is 5 feet high,
Ponch flew over like an avenging angel,
dropped right into the lilies of the valley,
picked himself up and dragged Wojo
off Lucky in the midst of the nastiest
caterwauling you could hear!
Because Wojo
had what he wanted,
free of the leash for a few hungry moments,
he went for manhood and hunting,
he pushed all his instincts into
that one big chomp on Lucky,
he was not about to let go,
to get all that meat and fur
in his teeth, and one good velvet ear,

the great bites he'd twitched about
for years in his dreams,
was not going to let that go.

But Ponch dragged Wojo off—
just when Heaven was ready
to call out Lucky's name—
didn't even feel the pain
until later.
Turned out Ponch cracked
a rib to break up the great cat battle.

You think just because male cats
don't have all their parts
they lose their fight but nothing
could be further from the truth,
this was to the death between these two.

I guess the passing of time
takes the hiss out of most everybody
but this 'ol war cat Wojo sniffing the breeze
is still looking for a last fight.
From the looks of things
it'll be coming soon
and Death is gonna have
some claw marks on it,
for sure.
As for Ponch,
he's one big-hearted man,
nursing Wojo right up to the edge,
and one fine neighbor
breaking himself up like he did
for our cat.

You can take *that* story
to the newspapers.

Big, Holy Arms

My friend,
maybe you mean something different
than me by the Holy Ghost
so let me say
I mean no disrespect
when I tell you
I just want something mysterious
and big and powerful
as the Holy Spirit
to take me over,
to carry me forward,
shake me into a new feeling,
because, well, it's hard to tell you,
but I've sprung a leak.

I have a secret.
Maybe you want to know
what, or why,
maybe you could care enough
to ask me,
what I need,
what I'm looking for,
something to stir my spirit,
manifest some beauty in me,
wake me up divinely.

Why?
Come on, come on, I dare you
to know how much I need some salvation,
just a touch of it.
See, I knew it,
you're gonna back off now
aren't you, turn away your eyes,

you think I'm begging,
too raw, too loud. Ask too much of you,
what if you just got close enough
to find out what it is,
this feeling I'm after,
No, you got to come closer than that,
You can't find out from that distance,
this is something you got
to get down on your knees
to see in me,
look real deep
and take your time.
Let me know I can
trust you,
yeah, that's it,
Now maybe now I can tell you
what I'm dying for,
I've got to reveal,
can't go out to everybody now,
but I have to tell you
how much the old feeling,
the feeling I always counted on,
how it dies in my arms sometimes,
you see, it's faith, faith that's
leaking out of me,
bleeds from wounds in my ears,
all the wrecked bodies
all over the streets
the bitter secrets of home,
bullets in the breeze,
all the wasted trees,
all this bad feeling around here,

all this bad news.

Yes, come close so I can whisper,

I'm losing it,
somedays I haven't got the little button
inside me like before,
the "things will get better" button,
the "we're gonna work it out" button,
it's hard to admit this,
this not enough of it, not enough faith attack,

And what about you, my friend,
you used to believe in change,
but look at you,
you're heading back into your own life
like you have the privilege
to walk away from the world,
you, you, of all people,
it scares me, I scare myself, so many backs
turning away, ice build up in the heart,
so many backs,
turning, everyday people, turning away,
but I've got to come back to myself,
can't point the finger anywhere but here,
here's all I know, and somedays I'm weak,
I'm failing,
so now that you're with me,
my friend,
Yes, I need you next to me,
I want you to witness me,
right now, because I'm going
to call on Faith,

Faith, can you hear me
can you stir me up
with some new feeling
to go on, to go ahead,
Faith, tell me giving up is too easy,
tell me despair—my own, is too early,

Faith, ask the tough questions,
like "Have you gone down hard enough
to be hopeless?"

I know, I know, everybody's got

to know their own moment
when despair takes them,
when they've seen too much,
heard too much,
suffered, suffered,
but please, send on down, or up
bring on over here
and move me, us
stir us all of us who need
something big and mysterious
and ghostly,
sweep us from within
with your big, holy arms.

Prayer For A Worried Child

*Thin little girl, age six: "I'm going on a diet
because my tummy is too fat."*

Little girl, with an early
troubled mind
water-lily blossom child
already tinged with ghosts
and gloom,
may your fears for your beauty,
more ancient than you can imagine,
fall away, away,
down the steep side of night
into the wide lap of mercy,
may moon flowers
that glow only in darkness
alight in your dreams.
Little one,
may you waken
to the morning-blessing
of your precious
perfect body feeling
at home,
safe
while we pray
for our mad world
and for you:
dear Goddesses, and—
if you're listening—Gods,

*Please return
to this haunted girl
her childhood.*

The Gospel According To Pie

Brothers and sisters—I bring you big news from the
universe. A PIE. At this moment, hot blueberry-peach
pie is coming out of Jan's oven like the steamy angel of
love. Can you feel it? The pie is a calling, a summons to
gather in shared acts of delight. Ed, the happy spouse of
pie-creator Jan, is even as we speak, taking out from the
ice-box the Mountain Valley Vanilla Custard to soften to
the peak of creaminess.

Gradually friends arrive, following the tug toward the
kitchen. A small collection of humans, on some day in
the country—this is news, you're thinking? This tiny
event? Just five unknowns—Ricardo, Lou, Robin, and,
of course, Jan and Ed. Midwestern, yet.

Who are they? They are simply having pie together in
the midst of an indifferent world-at-large. Yet does any
of them realize their own possible insignificance, the
sheer ordinariness of joy they are about to experience?
No. Does the rush of Time, the promise of Mortality
seem to haunt them? No. They share the same
properties as stars of the solar system, including the
sun—they give off more light and heat with each passing
year.

Actually there will be two pies, and everybody knows it,
though no one actually reveals this fact out loud. There
is mystery here. Chuck, the cat, feels it. He is home-
bound now, an indoor cat. Why? To protect him from
the hunters' traps in the deep woods that killed his
running mates. He chews at the hair on his legs. This is

his habit, as he tries to domesticate his wild nature.
Ready to pounce on enchantment, he sticks close by the
table, with his ears up.

Can you imagine how the first pie slides onto the table.
Everyone is tuned to the edge of their senses, in a
heaven especially intense for it is to be shared right
there in the full voyeurism of mid-day. Yes, not even a
hint of darkness falling. Outside Spring threatens to
come prematurely in thunder and lightning. Cardinals
thrill the air. Inside the friends sit so close their thighs
emanate heat beneath the table, and when someone says
something funny or teases, they bump for a moment as
they laugh—a quiver of molecules generating affection.

Steadily the vanilla custard makes the rounds and each
has their own way of placing ice cream on their slice,
some off to the side so it will slowly slide into the pie,
others plop it right on top, going for immediate contact.
Slowly they move toward the first touch. Soon there is a
silence broken only by raptures of ooohs, sighs, long
gazes into each other's eyes, then "O, Jan, O, Jan"
breaks from their lips as "Yes, Yes," for without her pie,
this moment would have been forever lost to them, and
they know it.

Chuck, the cat, joins them by chewing off more of the
hair on his lower legs as if they are covered with
hummingbird tortes—or sardines. He stalks his legs,
then savors them until they are wet and naked.
Everyone is eating.

*At this same moment, and before the second
pie, two more of the world's species will be*

driven to extinction; the frogs' eggs of Spring-
Time in America will begin to bake in the
over-exposed sun and perish beneath the torn
sky, every twelve seconds violence takes down
a woman, 2 kids will die this half hour from
gunshots, prisons forge the new slavery, while
certain scientists who prefer other worlds now
happily assure us there are actually ten
dimensions, not a mere three, and the world is
spinning at 700 miles per hour.

But these friends, just now, are beyond the Big Picture. They are in space. The space between longing and connection—special Midwest kitchen sensations only known among long-time friends in the blended presence of each other and pie. Softly melted ice cream seeps between bites, loosening the warm slice into a rush beyond words. Each can feel the temperature slowly cool in the final moments from which they look up, shyly, satisfied enough, in the pause between pies, to search the gooey remains of their intelligence for some sociable comment that might redeem them. But why bother, everyone's cheeks are flushed, their eyes warm, their timing perfect, simultaneous, vulnerable, all together.

Each knows, somewhere deep, that this love is ecology, a direct service to creation. On this good afternoon, they are an Environmental Protection Act as practical as crushing cans, lowering emissions, or sending money to the rainforests. *Each is Earth to the other, and the pie is GRAVITY.*

The vibrations of cherishing one another take off on a flight plan that touches any air, water or hardened heart in its path with the jet stream of appreciation. This is not the firm-lipped lesson of suffering, or the heavily celebrated School of Hard Knocks. This, Brothers and Sisters, is the Gospel of Soft Love Pats which also, yes, believe it, deepens the soul and makes the world safer.

Outside the kitchen, the surrounding land, and above, the sky, imminent buds and wakening bees sing praise songs for these humans who are home for each other.

True, they had witnessed differences of values and style come up. Ed had said to Ricardo, *"How can you possibly not like ice cream with pie—is that normal?"* Ricardo responded: *"Well, it's too wet and sloppy your way."* Despite this bitter difference, they had not gone outside for a duel, these two men, and while the whole outdoors waited with baited breath, Ed resolved the conflict. *"Oh,"* he responded, and smiling, said, *"Guess that just leaves more ice cream for me!"* And it was over. Unbelievable. Two opposing truths had survived together in the company of humans.

The entire back yard and its creatures relaxed in relief—for them this was truly an Earth Day, a call to celebrate. One despairing goldfinch took the risk to go off Prozac, frog families by the pond dared to imagine the future, and the early bees stopped doing too much honey amongst the daffodils.

Sure, the creatures knew from their ancestors that earth would go on even if humans did themselves in and took

a piece of all of life down with them. An elder among the wildlife would remind them that every 100 million years, or so, a small planet the size of Mount Everest, moving at sixty times the speed of sound smacks into Earth with unimaginable devastations. Do you know there have been 30 such hits since the start of life? Not to mention that eons ago oxygen came to this world like an apocalypse, as a ghastly pollutant that annihilated most of creation. Can any destruction humans do compare—in the Big Picture? Earth recovered from each catastrophe. She was stimulated to create all sorts of new life forms and species—like all of us.

Backyard prophets among the creatures speculated that the truly Final End to Earth might even lie beyond the capacity of humans. An ancient Sugar Maple would preach,

> *"My friends, think of the Big Bang theory. All elements once swirled together into a hot and compressed egg, a Primeval fireball which then exploded out to form one hundred billion galaxies rushing through space. The universe has been unfolding ever since. Will it keep on expanding? Perhaps even now it has reached a fever pitch and is preparing to Snap Us Back into a steamy egg that will cook up the next world. Not to mention, the heating up of the sun's fire has put our Earth in the 11th hour of her natural life."*

So, Brothers and Sisters, everything passes. Humans in the big picture are not as scary or so powerful. Why, we

know now they are so much empty space that any human, compressed into actual matter, will fit into one tablespoon.

But who lives every ordinary day, every ordained day, in the big picture? Can you live every moment with your eye on the whole ball of wax back through the millennia? Not Jan and Ed's backyard. These creatures are alive right now and care for humans as companions on earth in their daily rounds. They have faith in us even if we do only add up to a tablespoon. They know many people believe that in our deepest nature lies a sting, a murderous seed of the future; many people believe that the thing branding us human is the tool, and the thumb that grasps and cocks to kill.

But the backyard's major historian, the old Maple, knows for a fact that the dominant act of early humans was food-sharing, not greed and killing. So it excited hope among the wildlife and environment all around to see these friends re-enacting the generous fount of their early nature. They know Ed is reaching deep into the origins of being when he heads for the freezer and says, *"I'll get us another quart of custard."* As he opens its cold, tight cover with his opposable thumb, he moved the Elder Maple to a special ceremonial toast reserved for these moments: *"The universe shivers with wonder in the depths of the humans."*

So in the pause before the second serving, all around them, creation basked in the presence of these delicious folks who were again about to practice safe pie and mellow ice cream.

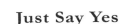

Just Say Yes

"In the face of uncertainty,
hope is a viable alternative."
Author Unknown

Any renewal becomes possible
just as day spills into evening
in this constant shift
of earth's shadow,
we are new forms
evolving in her waters,
fired in her kiln
each day,
any renewal become possible
as the light shifts
while the evening salmon sky
swims toward the west
to spawn,
leaving behind
the gift of birth
in the downstream
currents of dawn,

any renewal becomes possible,

just say
YES

YES!

"Whisper to the silent earth—I am flowing,
To the flashing water, say I AM."
Rainier Marie Rilke, Sonnets to Orpheus

The Day The Story Arrived

Over the years, I got so I could tell when the sky was ready. I wouldn't let sleep catch me! I liked to imagine the snow was already gathered in the Big Dipper and some shooting star would come along and tilt it, just for a moment, so the snow would spill out and bring Grandma's story with it.

Then Grandma'd find me staring out my window at the sky way into the night. "I could just feel you still up, *Tommy,* just pushing that story before its time, stubborn as you are!" she complained. And just for fun I'd press her, "Oh, couldn't you just tell it right now, tonight" and she'd say "Doll Baby, now you know as well as I it's too soon for that story. Let me tell you something. Some tales are for every day, or any season. But this one has its time, and that's only when the first snow comes. Even you can't make that story happen before then. You got to learn that some things are even bigger and stronger and more headstrong than boys."

"Like what, Grandma?"

"Like for instance, Mother Nature. So you just get in bed and run some of that restlessness out of you in your dreams. The leaf does not fall far from the tree, you're just like your Daddy was at your age."

I wished secretly now that Grandma wouldn't call me Doll Baby. I'm too old. She even said the other day that I'm taking on the voice of a man, although to me I just sound pitiful, like a broke-down piano with keys missing.

missing. I'd just as soon say nothin' for about a year.

"O. K., Grandma," I say with this tone I know gets a rise out of her. It's my best tool against older people and weather and even stories that always seem to know more than me. Maybe I'm too grown up now anyhow. Shouldn't act like I care so much about a dumb story, it's unmanly to be excited and all. Thing is about this one, it wasn't like a kid's story that belonged to everybody. This story didn't even exactly belong to Grandma, on account of how it made you and her wait for just the right time for the telling. It's as if it had its own life and a stubborn mind, and I like to pit it against mine. So I'd watch the weather, smell the air, follow the clouds to guess the day the story would arrive.

Grandma would see me sniffing and always say, "Honey, it's like a surprise visit from an old relative—there's just a mysterious moment when the sky decides to unfold its winter linens and shake out the first snow. And there's no telling just when that's going to be."

I wait and wait, every year, aiming to catch that moment, and then when the very first flakes start to fall, I run to her, "Grandmother, tell me again the story."

Still she teases me, "Now which story do you mean?"

"You know," I say, "about the red fox and his mate."

"Well," she says, and she puts her plump, ancient and soft hand on the over-stuffed worn-out easy chair. She snugs herself back into it, but it's only when she scruffs her bedslippers together that I know for certain she's going to say, "Now that's a true story. This weather, and the long nights, well, they just take me back."

In that moment she threw another log on the fire burning inside me for her to begin. I watch the snow fall and gather again outside, and inside the story.

"There was a red fox, you see, and he had a mate, and the two of them roved and hunted together side by side for two years, through the woods and meadows near our house on Storm Creek. These foxes they were a sight to see together, especially in winter, like red lightning that flashed across the pale fields. They lived in a burrow beneath the wood pile out near that big old lilac tree you liked to hide under."

I could see Grandma was settling into the tale, the way she rubbed her feet together on her bunions like they helped her remember. In fact, her slippers were real shiny right there along the big toe, just from stories.

Grandma was saying, "Now if you've ever seen a red fox out in the snowy fields in sunlight, you probably do remember its coppery-bright fur and fine, plush tail. It was in their second year together that the female just disappeared—I didn't see them on their usual runs together. Right away, I told your Grandad, used as we'd gotten to see them out there together—'Something's not right, Pa, the way that fox is out there now alone.' At night your Grandad and I would be in the big room with just the fire lit." Here Grandma would always pause, and I was sure I could see shadows of that fire on her

face, and I know by how she was looking far away with
her eyes she was seeing Grandpa like they were then,
settled on the big couch that looked out over the land.

"Well, a few weeks passed, and we began to see the red
fox running across our front lawn in the moonlight—
back and forth, back and forth. Then, even stranger,
he'd rear up sometimes on his hind legs pawing the night
air. We watched and watched, wondering, and your
Grandad said, "Lina, I do believe it's his loneliness.'
One night as I opened the front door, our tom cat
Zachary came streaking toward us from the yard.
Following Zach was the red fox dead on his heels, barely
a tail hair separating them! They ran into the room
before I could shut the door. It was a mystery—why
ordinarily that fox would just never have taken after that
big old cat."

Here Grandma let forth with a slow, rolling sound deep
in her that always came with this part of the story, and
she rubbed hard on her slippers. "Why, if it was food
that fox was after," she hooted, "Zach'd be tougher than
an old hide. Was hardly nothin' could put fear in that
kitty! But Zach was a mess of fright, his tail pointed
toward heaven like a steeple, indicating serious life and
death points of view. That fox stopped against the wall,
throwing a great shadow, completely flummoxed that
he'd really ended up in here, right next to us. Then he
stretched his throat back, letting loose with a sound I'd
never heard, like a lost, haunted bird of the jungle.
When his voice trailed off, the cracking of fire in the
room was the only sound. I was so struck, I just stood
at that open door—he streaked out just as sudden and

headed for his burrow in the wood pile.

Well, I looked at your Grandad who was looking at me, and he said, 'DadGummit, if I don't think that fox has visited us with a message.' " Grandma took a moment here—like she was listening to him, my Grandpa, only this time she took longer to say what always came next, and I couldn't wait, so I said, "Grandpa sure knew how to figure things, didn't he, Grandma." 'Cause that's always how she put it. "Yes, honey, yes he did." And I don't know why she had tears at this part of the story— she didn't usually except maybe hearing those words come from me about Grandad, it felt different. Maybe, too, she realized how hard I'd been listening all these years.

No one had bigger handkerchiefs than Grandma—hand-made and she'd embroidered her initial at each edge—a large, strong "A" for Angelina. She always had one around in her pockets and once I got older I'd tease her, "Those are big enough for a spaghetti dinner, Grandma!"

"That's how I designed 'em, honey—'Cause you can't have any kind of good cry with those puny lace things they make for ladies. One nose blow and they're finished, and I'd have to use my apron."

She didn't just dab her eyes. No, Grandma would pause to mop her whole face during her story-telling. There was no hurrying her, either, until she'd composed herself, and if I'd get excited and urge her to go on she'd say how life wasn't always about to go at my pace. And stories were as good a place as any to learn that.

So after she'd recovered, finally, she would say, "Next

So after she'd recovered, finally, she would say, "Next morning after the red fox paid us a call, it had snowed the first snow after a hard frost. I and your Grandad went out to the wood pile to find the burrow. When I probed the branches and logs, ice snapped with small clicking sounds. Then the red fox scrambled up, we jumped back, and it just fled, streaking away into the meadow. But something made me go back to that spot, I could feel it in me, put my ear down. I could hear small whelping cries below the surface—Have mercy, the red fox had a brood! Kits, they call 'em. I can tell you, your Grandad was way more upset than I'd seen him in a good while, 'Ma,' he said, 'His mate must have died. Maybe some fool even shot her for a God Danged coat, here this fox is all by himself to provide.'

"When I pulled them from the den, only one was dead. I still remember the warmth of their quivering red bodies in my arms, against my chest, like feathers with a heart beat."

And always I say, even though I know—"Really—babies, Grandma?" And she says, "Oh, we rescued them and nursed 'em good." My heart and my eyes just fill up, and then all choked up, I go on to say "What happened to the dead one, Grandma?" Except this time before I could get a word in, she just went right on and said "Honey, you got a real big heart, like your Granddad, and don't you ever forget it, because a lot of cold winds gonna blow your way to harden you just because you're a man." I could see she was going for her hankie again, and I didn't know what to do with myself so I just picked up the old way and said, "What happened to the dead one, Grandma?"

I always love this part and feel sad, too. "Your Grandad dug a small deep hole not far from the Creek—didn't think we should bury it so close to the burrow. Your Grandad and I, you know we got all teary-eyed over that tiny fox, you'll not see many things so sweet as it was, and never had a chance. All the rest would've soon followed, that's for sure. Your Grandad never talked too much about death. He even hated to hunt, though he did when money was lean. But after we buried that little dear baby, he said: 'Guess we're lucky to get so old, Ma.' "

Grandma was pretty much through even her handkerchief by the time she said, "And I'll never forget how he looked at me that morning, 'I hope I go before you, Angelina, because I just couldn't bear to be as alone as that fox out there last night.' "

Grandma looked out the window, real quiet. Like always. The story paused here a long time. The silence from all the other years drifted down on us, as though some day, she would just stare out the window forever, and the story would have to carry on without her. Finally, she said: "Our red fox never came so close again. Only a great desperate caring had brought him in with Zachary. As for that cat, well, some of his tail hairs never did lie down flat after that night. He had no idea he was important as the North Star for that wild creature. I'm sure Zach headed way up in the fields anytime the fox showed himself near the house again. And some nights, he did. We'd see him running up and down the yard, crying out in his strange voice, lifting up on his hind legs. I wished there was some way to tell

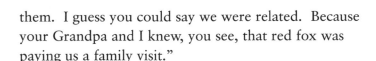

them. I guess you could say we were related. Because
your Grandpa and I knew, you see, that red fox was
paying us a family visit."

I never did find out what happened to those little fox
kits. Grandma never said, and I just like to think
Grandma and Grandpa returned them to the red fox
after they'd grown enough to make it on their own.
Don't know though. Lots of Grandma's stories sort of
have no ending. She'd say to use my imagination. I used
to want to know the details, and the final truths and all.
But she'd say, "Honey, you can't track down everything.
Trying to find words for magic is like lighting a fire with
water. There's times you're better off just letting things
be." You were as likely to get something more out of her
as the sky would give up its secrets.

So I knew this moment, when she said the red fox was
kin, was as far as the story would go—ever. It used to be
the time, when I was littler, that Grandma pulled me all
the way onto her lap. I'd feel her girth surround me like
warm mittens spun from the softest wool. There was
just nothing like being swept up by Grandma, her whole
body was another story holding me fast as the year
started to turn cold.

I know why the red fox found her. And I know why
Grandpa passed first. Life without her, well, I imagine
it'll be like the Big Dipper just fell out of the sky.

Hard Road

Hard Road

Odd sensations. Rotofsky was wondering. When did
they begin? These strange sensations in his legs, his
arms, mysterious visitations from inner space. The first
time he'd noticed, it seemed hot. July, maybe. On a day
like today. Last summer. Almost a year ago—how did a
year pass between these two days? His head felt thick,
somehow apart from his body, floating above the block
like a sooty moon waiting for its time to rise, later, in a
clearer sky. Now the air hung low—ozone alert, sun
shone so hard on Center the street looked bald and pale
with a faint fuzz like after chemotherapy. Like the
block, Rotofsky felt his whole life needed a wig to create
the appearance he was alright. Because somehow he
was not, this he almost knew. It was dead on high noon
with the siren wailing.

Recently his son had asked him, "Daddy, why does the
siren go off at noon?" Rotofsky said, "It's an angry
monster, Billy, screaming because it still has to work
seven more hours before it can lie down and rest."

Already the hot workday had gone on for too long.
He'd torn up his thumb again, real good this time.
Another medical opportunity. Go to the Emergency
Room. You're there bleeding in full view of the window
lady, she's whining, "Do you have an insurance card,
Sir?" You decide to kill her right there because she will
get immediate medical attention. You get stitched up.
200 bucks. Everyday was the possible onset of a
medical bill for him—drills, sharp metal, ladders at steep
angles, all carried that chance. So this time he mopped

blood himself. Push ahead, push ahead. There's the
next job. Well, he'd rely on his other hand, put on a
bandage. His thumb hurt like hell.

His next client was an Arab restaurant that needed some
adjustments on the iron work he'd put in last week. He
looked forward to seeing Habeeb because he was always
a good challenge, had some life to him. "How much you
charge me," he'd say. Rotofsky would answer, "$150."
"What. Are you kidding? You think I can afford that
here. I'm just a small business man." Rotofsky: "$125.
That's my lowest." Habeeb: "Cousin, Cousin, you got
to give me a break—who else is going to take care of
Middle-Eastern relations." Once Rotofsky had called
Habeeb "Brother," and Habeeb had said, "We're not
Brothers, we're Cousins," "Yeah, I know," said Rotofsky,
"we both got Abraham on our side." Now he replied,
"$175, *Cousin*." Habeeb laughed "$120—O.K. and
lunch." "Deal," Rotofsky shook hands to seal the trust
of friendship and businesss.

He always knocked off close to 50 bucks. Habeeb had
the best babaganooj around, thick with parsley and
garlic. They'd sit over dark heavily sugared coffee and
philosophize about the world, sometimes just sit in the
quiet. These moments saved his day from the loneliness
of riding all over town from client to client, except for
the radio. Often the music just got on his nerves so he'd
search for a talk show to distract him on a particularly
long ride. But all their bitter racist trash talk just made
him feel worse, a nasty soot that stuck to him in the heat.

Last month he'd installed a whole set of wrought iron railings inside Habeeb's restaurant along with the doors. They were strong, original railings with large, decorative clusters of grapes. All the time feeling strange again. He would look up at the scene on the wall of camels and limitless desert, get lost in the sands, the space, the light—until Habeeb or Samir would call something out to him from the kitchen, as unaware as he that he was travelling. He would return to his drill, powerful in his hands. Only after he'd finished the job did he notice the clusters of grapes were upside down and pointing skyward. He hoped no one would notice—they still looked good. But Samir came up a week later and said, "Hey, Rotofsky, how come Habeeb's grapes are upside down?"

He'd replied. "Samir, they aren't upside down. Habeeb's grapes grow up towards God." But he knew he was pushing it too far. Samir looked at Rotofsky, silent for a moment, then threw his head back with a big laugh, "That's a good one Rotofsky."

He left the restaurant feeling he'd got a good price for the repair. That would easily cover some bills. When he got back into his truck, he felt stuffed, especially in the heat. There was no air conditioning in his truck except the hole in the floor where you could see right down to the asphalt. Also the tiny black plastic fan he'd mounted right behind the steering wheel. He flipped it on, felt the hot mix of air, city and his own breath balloon around him. He sat there leaning both arms on the steering wheel. They'd fed him too well, these cousins.

Got to push on—next job. His thumb, his entire hand, was throbbing now. The whole back of the truck seemed to sweat. Every nail, screw, piece of twine, ready for toil, ready for his hands to give them their place in the world. His hands were their reason for living. He could feel them all back there, his travelling companions who he spent more time with than his family. His tools. Nails, blades. It started way back when someone figured out fire, his future was in that first friction, that spark that created all this metal, these sharp surfaces, his strength. His son could chin himself on one of his arms. His arms were bulldozers pushing towards his nicked, scarred tools for hands.

He felt again the strange sensations, just now in his legs. He went to turn on the truck. Forget the radio. There it was—that feeling in his legs. Was it something pushing him from behind? He had to get going. He could lose this next job if he didn't do the estimate. The ledger in his mind told him he needed it to replace his old drill press. His legs felt scary, somehow moving in a circle. He should go, get going, get the truck going. Even his good hand felt stubby and numb. Hard to grasp the keys. Something was the matter with him. Shaking it off he looked out. The four street corners were oily and dank like the armpit of workshirts at the end of the day. A large crow picked at something near a corner. Took off slowly, looking for a tree. Rotofsky watched it circle. Flying low, it was looking for a tree to rest in on the blighted corner. He couldn't take his eyes off its search. Rotofski knew this neighborhood—even here it would find tree. This bird was tough.

4 o'clock. Maybe he'd go do that estimate, but try and
knock off by 5. His hand throbbed, his hands, he'd
washed them before lunch. Now they had carbon from
Habeeb's receipts on them again. He held them up.
First, ink, then down a layer, oil, always oil. Faint smell
of gasoline. He stared at his hands. His Dad, when he
was alive, would always put his head down on his hands
and take a nap after he ate dinner. His Dad's hands
were never quite clean from work and when he'd pick
up his head off them, the hair on the backs would be
damp, leaving a pink imprint where his face had rested,
his fingernails nicked, full of grit. Rotofsky had never
understood those hands. Now he was looking at them.
He wanted to put his head down on his steering wheel
and wake up back then, after dinner, and he and his Dad
would go fishing together for the next twenty years.

There were so few times to remember because his Dad
was always working, pushing up dollars into the soil of
his family. Good dirt. Basic toil. Unending service. On
those rare times his Dad would say,

> *"Hey, pal, we're gonna go fishing tonight,"*
> *they would leave a few hours after dinner.*
> *Around 10 or 11 they would go into the dark,*
> *with their fresh live earthworms, and their*
> *fancy flies and hooks. It was such a strange*
> *break from their routine that it felt like a*
> *secret midnight voyage only God could set up*
> *for them. For one night they were the*
> *Chosen, going to the waters. They would*
> *drive to Port Washington along the roads*

before the Freeway and its pale fast lanes were built. God had especially provided the constellations and half-moon of a clear autumn night. They arrived and went into the company of other men and boys in the slip behind Jones Fish Market. Men's cigarettes would flicker in the night and the hum of conversation among sons and fathers blurred with the whir of rods and reels. White bobbers rode the blue-green waves in the close cloud of fog that wrapped around them.

One night a fish hook had torn into his same thumb hurting him now. He learned then what the fish felt and the earthworm. What it is to be bait while life swings its line out just for you and reels you in. Because even God on a good night can't stop the hook. But that night his father bandaged his wound, with the fascinating and reassuring way he had of being able to continue holding onto his cigarette, smoking it at the corner of his lips, even while he used both hands to clean and bind him up.

"You're gonna be OK, pal," his Dad said. Then they drove home in the dawn, perch and catfish swimming in the pail, so his father could get right back to work from sun-up until dinnertime, when, after some great fish broiled in butter, finally he'd put his head down on his hands and sleep.

A harsh street noise shook Rotofsky awake. He jerked his head up off the steering wheel. Checked the time— his watch stared up at him with its big hand, its little hand, with its tiny alarm that worked under water. The call of the work day was all crammed into that little face that even glowed in the dark. Something strange was happening to him.

His head was full of crows. He could still hear his Father's voice. *"You're gonna be OK, pal."*

Rotofsky thought, "From your lips to God's ears, Pop."

My Name's Adriano. But What's It To You?

San Francisco, 1995

You want to know why I'm leaving this city? First, let me begin with the melancholy that comes over me when I talk about my life, plus who I am—my name, what you can call me, since we've just met, is Adriano. "Is that Mexican?" you ask. So now you want to know already *"What kind of a name is that?"* You mean, *"What am I?"* You mean, what blood flows in me? You don't even know me and you want the inside information. You know, you shouldn't go deep so fast, you won't have anything left. Wait awhile before you ask the Blood questions. But hey, this is America, you want to know who you're talking to, right?

Anyway, let me go back to my mood upon leaving, the sadness of departing from this city I've bared myself to, a great city that has not yet learned to love me. Yeah, I'm moving on from here where it's the law now if you're a beggar like me you have to beg softly so you don't scare the "haves" with your "have not." Speak up too loud, wave your little white cup too vigorously— busted. So yeah, definitely I want to go on to a place where I can fall on my knees in front of, say, a pretty woman who's carrying her bags full of purchases she doesn't even need, probably about to go to dinner in a restaurant with great lighting, and sit before a glass of dark wine, red and healthy that soon will warm her deep inside, but before she walks in that door I don't want to just quietly shake my white cup and mumble at her. I mean, listen, if you want me to *meditate* out here on the corner, well, some things I don't do in public, believe it or not. But this city got its hand on my mouth.

Gag order. So I'm gonna head out, to some other town, so when I see such a lady as I mentioned coming toward me I can call out loud and proud—*"Ma'm, can you give me some spare change."* Then see how she pulls her bags close, keeps moving fast but I keep coming at her, lowering into a fast crouch, 'til right when she's gonna pass me I bring on the final cry, I fall to my knees, hold out my black hat and plead inches away from her skirt just before she passes: *"I'm begging you. Think of my children!"*

Then I watch her back, her *fleeing* back but I know I gave it my personal best.

So that's why I'm leaving this city with its little white cup policies, its politeness with no mercy, a city that closes me down. No more. Adriano is moving on.

"So what kind of a name is that?" Is it Italian? still you ask. Greek? It's still big in your mind, after all this, what ethnic group I belong to, my roots, my ancestors? Well, I'm just like you—one of the Boat People, yeah, one of my Ancestors decided to come here to America, they came off the boat to be free! Somebody cut off just the tip of their name to make them American, and here's the end of the family line. Me. Who can't beg too loud. Oh, I have rights. I have the right to beg in a whisper.

So you want to place me? Then call me from the tribe of **"Those who beg in a loud voice."**

And now you also want to know how come I'm so "articulate". I was in Nam—graduated right to war. And guess what, too? Vietnam made me a poet. Words caught fire in me. Maybe you'd like to hear one of my poems, surprised as you look, they liked this at our readings in "Homeless Park"—check it out.

> They pulled me into Vietnam
> so soon after college
> you could say the jungle
> was my graduation ceremony.
> It was a hot time.
> Nam burned me into a poet.
> I learned to swallow words,
> blade and all, then bring them
> back up still in flames.
>
> I lost so many brothers.
> I learned to stare into the trees
> a thousand yards
> and hear the enemy
> with my eyes.
>
> My whole body
> learned to see—
> I was a burning light
> for my country.
>
> Still, back home in Golden Gate USA
> they tried to turn me into
> a falling down,
> burned-out star,
> a voiceless beggar.

Some of my lights are out,
but I'm still
on fire
for all of us.

Looking Good

Frankie was just sitting. Sitting in the Greenwich Cafe
"musing"—that intense luxury of doting on your own
mind. That delicious course of revelations as you thread
your life through the eye of the body, in solitude.
Frankie was unleashing free and uncloistered outbursts
of mind-play, as when a monk strips off his robes and
goes skinny-dipping. Frankie was out of time, she was
through with time. She had started off reading the *N.Y.
Times* and ended up tossed by reveries that lifted her
like the old carnival's ferris wheel one summer reeled
her into the sky. Then held her there at the top, flung
over the night. These days, musing put her at that edge,
with all the hawkers out to sell her memories until she
could smell the past like it was in her pocket. She had
burst the veil of time and space. She was all the
amusement park rides at once, she had already speeded
through the Tunnel of Love and ended up in the Fun
House.

Frankie was musing—calling forth the House of
Mirrors. She was on a big ride now, and she knew if she
did not have a body to hold her, her life would pass on
with the speed of light. People looking at her would still
see a glow, when, like a star, she'd long ago burned out.
If not for this body of hers, she'd just be one mind-flash
following another into oblivion. She supposed she
should thank this slow clay. Yes, her old body was the
anchor: once the obsession of her youth, next, the
ambivalent companion of her various middle ages. And
now she was, according to the charts, simply old.

Oldness. This was a major new relationship, like adolescence, and her body had all sorts of developments and suggestions for her. As a teenager the Prom hovered in her fantasies of Spring and Love like a pluckable and reliable fruit. Now she thought of the Zen story of the man (of course) clinging to the side of a mountain, having slipped, alone, no one to save him. Clearly he will fall to his death. As he begins to lose his grasp he sees next to him a beautiful wild strawberry. He plucks it, and by doing so, he surrenders his grip on the mountain. As he falls, he savors its fresh taste: "Ah, what a beautiful fruit, this strawberry." Something immediate and vivid and sweet, something to burn for even as she slides towards the Eternal. Frankie was tasting the question—where, in old age, was the strawberry, the wild strawberry, for her?

She felt different now about death, she was realizing. Not fear. She was strong and well. Well enough— nothing a few pills couldn't handle. She had more of a sense that every day needed to be plucked, to be made much of. Each day was, in fact, increasingly grasping her and pressing her towards moods, ecstasies, envies and little revenges that she could not direct. Life was mulching up some new personality for her. So let her be the wild strawberry. So let life slide down the mountain, hang on by its teeth to her and take some good final bites.

Suddenly Jonathan appeared next to her, startling her, reeling her back to the cafe table. He grasped her arm, and his hands were vivid and strong. All his youth was in motion beneath his skin and heading somewhere.

"It's been so long, too long," he said. "I wanted you after my last concert! What happened to you?" He was dressed in a suede jacket, brown. A classy silk shirt with tucks just where they belong in his pants. All brown and beige, understated, so the vitality in his face burned even brighter.

"You shine!" she burst out. "And I just couldn't get at you that night, you were surrounded by so many people. Plus I'm always shy to go up on stage," she said. After his dance concerts, the air was full of sweat and excitement, raw—young.

He grasped her arm again and pressed it. "Feel it. I have energy! God, it's so good to see you. I've just choreographed for the Robert Jones Co. this afternoon. I'm doing it, I'm dancing and doing choreography all over the place. Listen, can you stay awhile?"

"Absolutely," she said and instantly their table in the dingy cafe light took them to the closeness their earlier connections had assured.

"I'm auditioning tomorrow off-Broadway—it's big. You always have the right words. I need you to help mellow me out."

Her hearing had worsened even more since they last met, and street sounds from the East Village through the huge cafe window blurred his voice. "Sit around by my good ear and let's catch up."

She felt the grace of his youth and her age together. She

felt again how their connection was one of the fruits of her elderliness. She felt his need for her. Each time they met, in the troubled times as well as now, she experienced how he could create an intimacy from the places where fire lives—and the muse. His heat enlivened her. His brilliance as a dancer and creator of dance could fill the classical forms and proprieties with the warmth of creative passion. He danced straight from the source.

"So performing's going well—not so scary as before?"

"Now I don't think of it as 'taking' or an ego thing, more and more I focus on what I can give."

She knew this but it was exciting to hear the thinking behind his artistic choices. He was deep, this one, no unexamined life here. She knew this because he used to move somewhat separate from his body, small gestures that made line and form impeccable but stayed on the ground. Since then something in him had broken loose. In this last concert his body flew along with his phrases, even his eyes reflected the moods and tone of each piece. He pierced the heart and lifted her, lifted them all. The audience called him back. Twice. In New York.

"Yes, I'm taking shape, I feel it will happen, my career will take off. I just focus on the future as much as I can. You know the old saying: 'If you don't change directions, you'll end up where you were heading.' "

It took her a minute to sort that one out. For a young person, he always was full of quotes. That quality was the same, and she could always feel his warmth, but this was a different Jonathan from a year ago and before. Then he was a chronic question, unsteady, with only moments when the center held. His personality registered like aftershocks. He would let hope fly into his hand, then he'd close down until it stung him like a yellow jacket. What might you expect? Then he was just 22. In search. On the outskirts of himself and the world.

Not to mention his early life. He'd sneak around his house like an outlaw, his face pale as vodka while his father threw around flower pots, screaming "Your Mother's a whore, you little piece of shit," so after his third birthday party he was turned over to an ancient malevolence passing for his grandmother who pushed his head underwater and would not let him up until he ceased all struggle, all movement. Life was as safe as a fox hole. How had he ever dared again to believe in movement. To dance. Clearly a victory of his soul—and a lot of help he'd opened to, later, due to some unfathomable trust he'd salvaged. She wanted to right the balance, so to speak. To be trust-worthy. She felt lucky he had anything to do with old ladies. She was practicing this word for herself—old. On the outside her body was carrying on visible and heavy discussions with mortality. Inside there was nothing that matched.

But Jonathan was saying to her, "So you, God, you look so good. You've lost weight or something!"

"Well, you know, you hit seventy you've got to work out!" She laughed on the outside. Quickly: "I belong to this Club near Central Park."

The weight loss comment evoked so many other weight loss comments. Just let her lose 10 pounds and the stir she created was staggering. Through the years of her ups and downs, people would approach with intense, hungry eyes—"God, you look good! What happened to you, you look so different—why, you look 10 years younger." *Thin.* Oh, joy, again she was freshly anointed, back on the map, ordained and valued, belonging to the Community. She was once again a loyal feature of the collective body like a classic nose.

Jonathan was saying, "Seventy! God, can you be 70— seems like just last year you turned 65." Actually she was 74.

"So, you were a kid when I met you and here you are, almost 30! You still look so young."

"Hey, I gotta look young. Young is good." Laughing sheepishly.

She gave him a look. She knew what that cue was about.

He knew she knew. "I do practice safe sex—big time. Really. You know, Frankie, I could get this virus again— every time you get exposed to this virus you can get it again in a new way."

"That is really scary."

"I can't believe how many people are just out here taking risks. Or they're afraid to get tested. Especially some of these young guys, they just don't care—nothing is real. I feel like I've got to help them, but I don't want to just always be focussing on this disease. That could take all of my energy."

"Jonathan, is it that they just don't know the facts, or what?"

"Well, I can relate, what did I know back then. So what if I was only 23, I already felt like damaged goods, I figured for someone like me the love of my life would never come and I just really wanted someone to get next to."

She added: "Well, that was the 80's, too. What did anyone know. Even the President couldn't bring himself to speak the word AIDS."

"That's true." He looked at her. "Thanks for saying that, Frankie. Anyway, I'm really careful. And real choosy. I'm just going boyfriendless right now. It's got to be right. Even dating—I go for months sometimes, just because I'm afraid, not only of me, but of someone else, what they'll go for, you know, in the moment."

"Yep," she said, "Lust has a life of its own."

He was hurt. Up to that point they'd been perfect and even with each other. "When you say it that way, well, it . . . . " He dropped it.

"What?" she asked.

"Well, LUST—the gay male, quick and dirty. You know,

coming from you, and you had this look on your face."

"Come on, give me a break, I've got nothing against lust," she said.

For a moment their little world spun back into reality, the cafe smelled of smoke, turned sour.

She realized he had opened to her quickly as always. Had she delivered a cheap shot? These days she could lose track with people and sting. Was she supposed to be the elder, peaceable one? All tenderness, and no messy feelings? Just wise and consoling statements?

"Listen, that wasn't against you, Jonathan—or lust. I know lust can have a life of its own—*I was thinking of my life*." There she had done it again, slipped on someone's words and fallen into the past. Whatever Jonathan wanted her to know about his life right now, she was somehow off on her own, to times when she just went for the moment without real intimacy. Not much relationship. She moved with one urge—to meet life's mouth, its deep thrusts. The embrace where sensation is the only responsibility you respect. She had lit many flames and blown them out when she felt like it. She missed those days, still felt the fire in her body. One day a big breath would blow her out. Lust knew this—about everybody.

She came out of it to see Jonathan still looked uncomfortable. With these time seizures, spinning out of the present, she was becoming a poor listener. Or was the past fusing with the present? Now just where had they left off? In a split second she decided that he

was having a hard time putting her together with sex,
like she and lust would be strange bedfellows. Well, she
was thinking that's what he's thinking. She was
remembering once when he'd called Barbara Walters "an
ugly old witch." He hadn't liked the provocative way
she had interviewed a gay athlete with AIDS.
Immediately he'd apologized when she called him on it.
Still she was angry. Not at him really, way past him, but
angry now.

"O. K., Jonathan, this young thing—I have to say
something about that. How can I say this?   Well, I
guess it upsets me because it's a big thing among
straights, too. You know that. Out with the old, on with
the young. But it seems like gay men are super into this
good body thing and I have a real attitude against that."
Even while she was speaking, part of her was thinking
"Frankie, Frankie, why now, drop it—the kid didn't
create the world."

"You think I'm into it," he said.

"I know you're into it."

She was not being Mom here. She was on dangerous
territory. She should shut up.

"It's true, but now more for my health, really. And for
my work, Frankie."

The atmosphere was stretched tight. He looked down,
at his hands, down at the floor, down. Then he said:
"You know when I was young and I first knew I was gay,
I hated myself and especially my body because that's

what made me gay, made me different. Or when I didn't feel disgust, well, I knew everybody else did, so it was the same thing." Then he looked up, right at her. "It felt like there was only one way to be alright—that was to look good, working out to look good, *awesomely good*. And then, it wasn't like for a woman, eventually she'd get a man if she was pretty enough, at least her looks would lead somewhere, like to a future. I didn't really expect to get love, I just hoped maybe people would admire me. While I was hiding inside, feeling even more like shit then when I was a little kid."

He was wound up, his lips tight. She was so into her own feelings about it she hadn't noticed until now as he looked at her how much the spell between them, his glow, had given way. He just looked disturbed. Far from mellow. He had come to her buoyant, in flight. She'd dragged him down. She knew how important it was to him not to stress his health with depression. His body is his instrument. Yet somehow she'd made him dig, she'd stirred the past, the wretched past, she couldn't let it alone. Come on, everyone, let's muck around and think about it, THINK ABOUT IT ALL, don't leave anything alone, let's go back to the scene of, let's not let a single shred of evidence off the hook about everyone's reality, Mrs. Inside Edition.

Incredible. Seventy years old. Well, seventyish. Mean and covered with the smut of guilt as good as ever.

They sat there. Like wind roughing up clear water, the silence was torn by the unspoken.

Another little hotflash of madness and unfinished

business. "Frankie," she thought, "say something to him about how you're an old fool." Several lines from an Indian poem for elder women ambushed her: "Now you are wise and can see water in dust, breath in the stone." Oh, sure, that described her like a kick in the head.

Once again, Jonathan grasped her out of her reverie, he had remarkable hands, hands like concerts, all his vigor ran through her, "Gotta go," he said. "Love you."

She wondered, was that a new angle to his face with her, not the same chumminess? She feared he wouldn't be open any more with her after today—she in her infinite wisdom.

There are two kinds of regrets. Minor regrets are when you wish you had done something, or not done something. But that's life, you say, you let it go. Major regret is looking back at the wrong move that changed everything. He did not need her to remind him of mean old women. If she had to face the spoiled fruit of their demise—major regret.

Then, ready to leave, he shifted back and said: "When we meet again, I want to hear about your lust." He spun the word with just a little edge.

A reprieve. They would make it. She got lucky. But she had to work with this accumulating information: in the slide down the mountain toward endlessness, she was not a beautiful wild strawberry to be savored. She was a ballistic strawberry.

She embraced him hard until all the lights went back on in her heart.

The fire shot back into him and he said: "And next time I see you, Frankie, I hope you'll still love me. Because I'm going to look good. *This good.*"

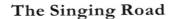

The Singing Road

Right now, the music is lonely,
looking for someone who cares,
yes, the music sings to itself,
searching, searching for a body
to make it real,
with its eye on the earth, the music
sends out
the call, the call for help
to touch down into the world.
Looking for somebody's dream,
it finds LaChance
with his mind and soul way open,
with just the right readiness
the music can trust.
Music sways above him,
waiting for that moment
to come down into him
and start the motion,
waiting for the veil to drop
between his skin and his dream,
so the music can fling
its way into sound
and wake a whole lot
of people up
with its gratitude.

LaChance was all stirred up like a bee doesn't know if
it's gonna sting or make honey. Right now summer
owned him, the music moved somewhere beyond his
grasp, and the concert was coming on fast. Heat had
gotten deep inside, even into his mind. He went down

to the basement, away from the hot, wet air, hoping to work on his piece for the Jazz Ensemble and generally lift himself up. Ended up playing the string bass just to cool out his head, think about how to arrange the instruments, had to work up his solo, write the ending which so far he had no ideas for. Even down here the heat found him, made the long strings slack beneath his hands, couldn't stay on key. He laid the bass down on its side. Even its curved, subtle body felt too close. They were both out of tune, out of touch. Definitely got to run this off. There was nothing that was not getting on his nerves, his fight with Julia, little big-mouth Jackie who he had tried to talk to, even Raheem was over the line. He went upstairs, put on some running shorts. He could taste the music in him like a sweetness but he had to get his mind clear to get at it. He should just stay in his neighborhood, get right back to the piece but he got in his car and drove over to run the lake, try to find a breeze.

Running purified him. He'd tell his little track team, "You got to get your muscles warm before you jump into it," but today he just went for it—just started running, stiff and slow at first, his whole body felt tired and weak. He looked up at the trees all leafed out, loose, in the green fullness of summer, and the lake carried his eyes all the way to the other side. He let the liquid space enter and move in him, soothe him, he ran slow, steady, running out the tightness, the hard words, the tears, and behind it all the piece pushing its way forward in him, trying to finish and fulfill itself. Along with it, he could hear an old song from way back ease into him, went something like, *"Let me come to the waters with my burdens, Lord, let me thank you before I die, let me come, Lord, to the water, please don't keep me from my gratitude.*" It was good, the music inside his head with its changes and textures, while he let Mother Nature's visuals slide over his tired eyes. He was stretched tighter than he knew. There was no breeze, only the wet close hands of the heat, no sound but inside himself, he could feel his breath pump his lungs, come in and out, the only wind stirring. The earth's pulse was weak in him, he kept running himself into the next level waiting for its response, waiting until he could feel its beat, kept on running, running until his body finally began to lay down a tempo, the road sang back to him, and his blood grew fertile with sound. A melody began to curl deep inside, innocent and new so his body had to cup itself to hear, like how he would stand early mornings listening to his sleeping children breathe, look out the bedroom window at the gracious trees with their angel wings shaking off a last dream into the green and blue, thankful. Mile after mile spilled off him, until he was lost and large, and beyond, he was the dreaming tree, the full-bodied summer dusted with a fine and golden pollen. He began, at last, to become clear, clear as the lake water pierced by light that travels all the way to the shadows, *"Please, ease my burdens, Lord."* The end of his piece started to come down into him, unfold in him, the changes came down, the tight harmonies called out, even tears of the hard and tender times poured into the music, and he knew what to do, he'd shift the whole last section into a minor key, push up the tempo so it moved, and he knew, he knew, he had what he needed to finish the tune, back in touch. He belonged. Only now did he realize he was hot, he was completely wet, close to over-heating. But light, very, very light. He slowed himself way down, felt freed now, ready for the concert. This piece was gonna walk tall with a headdress you could see for miles. The whole night would be a witness: *We're on a hard road, people, but it's a singing road.* The harmonies would stir up the audience in a way even the overhead fans, hard as they whirled, could not cool. Players would sweat the good sweat. The music would raise everyone up, and the gift that he hoped for would be delivered. Sounds of it and the liquid of his muscles, the whispering lake against the shore moved the water right up behind his eyes from way down in his heart. *Like clear, deep waters, music will make you whole.*